PerPETual Care

DISCLAIMER

This book contains important legal and financial information about the future of your pet. It is not intended to serve as legal and/or financial advice, only to provide examples of what is possible for some people in certain situations. For specific advice that is pertinent to your own situation, consult a legal and/or financial expert for personal assistance.

PerPETual Care:
Who Will Look
After Your Pets
If You're Not Around?

by Lisa Rogak

Litterature
Grafton, New Hampshire

Dedicated to all the beloved pets who were needlessly euthanized because their owners didn't plan for PerPETual Care

Table of Contents

Introduction

Two days before my deadline to send this book to the printer, I got a great lesson in why everyone who shares their home with cats, dogs, and/or other beloved pets needs to plan for their animals' future without them.

My friend and next-door neighbor died unexpectedly, leaving behind a two-year old mild-mannered but occasionally hyper dog named Dudley, who would show up at my back door every morning at 5:30 a.m. for his daily treat of Frosty Paws, ice cream for dogs. For me, it was as close as my cats would ever let me get to being a dog owner.

Neither Jack's daughter nor his son could take the dog, and so we began the mad scramble all surviving friends and relatives must go through to place an animal companion in another home when the owner neglected to make plans, calling local shelters, sanctuaries, asking friends if they could take the dog, even for a week or so while we worked to find him another home. I only wish I had written this book even six months ago, because then I could have nagged Jack about making arrangements for Dudley, despite the fact that his death was unforeseen. Instead, we're all frantically playing catchup and largely unsure of Dudley's fate.

Unexpected death and pets whose futures are unknown as a result are not isolated occurrences, and you don't have to be "old" to worry. The week before Jack's death, an email came across one of the pet rescue lists telling of a young woman who suddenly died at the age of 24, whose home was filled with rescued animals.

And then there are the breeders, professionals who make their livings surrounded by sometimes countless dozens of animals, and who surprisingly make no provisions for their future homes without them. An email from the grieving widow or widower then weaves its way through the rescue grapevine telling of the surviving spouse's inability to cope with the kennels or cattery, and then people all across the country are scrambling to find homes for fifty, sixty, or more animals, invariably in the middle of kitten and puppy season, no less, when shelters and foster homes are already filled to the brink. I'll bet that whenever you visit a shelter or go to an adoption event, you always look at the reason why each animal was surrendered by its supposedly lifelong owner. If you notice these things, you'll probably realize that "Owner entered nursing home" and "Owner passed away" seem to be appearing on adoptive animals' information cards more often lately.

As our population ages, this is bound to increase. Perhaps you've already found yourself in a similar situation, when a relative or friend suddenly died and it was up to you to find a new home for the animals left behind without concrete plans from the deceased owner. Or maybe you've worried about the fate of your own pets if something should happen to you; you know you should do something, but you're not certain about what you could do, and besides, all of that fancy estate-planning stuff is for other people, right?

Wrong. You need to make plans now to arrange for your pets' future care should fate unfortunately get in your way. Of course, it's unpleasant to think about your own demise, but it's even worse to consider where your beloved animals would end up if you were to suddenly disappear from their lives.

With your help, and a little work as outlined in this book, you'll be guaranteeing that your pets have a future if you're not around while reducing the number of pets that are abandoned to shelters.

1

Why You Need
PerPETual Care

In early spring of 2002, a man in Long Island who lived
alone died unexpectedly. Local authorities took care of
his body. His adult children arrived to make the funeral
arrangements and attended the services and burial.

A week after his death, his twelve adored cats remained
in his home, unfed, unwatered, uncared for.

When the man's son visited his father's house to pack the
items left in the house, he discovered the cats shut inside, all
in bad shape and some in need of medical attention due to
dehydration. The son, who was indifferent to animals at best,
didn't feel like dealing with the cats, so he opened the front
door to the house – located on a busy highway – picked up
the cats he could get his hands on and nonchalantly tossed

them out the door. He managed to throw only eight of the cats outside; the other four ran up to the attic to hide. His father must have rolled over in his grave.

Word about this appalling incident quickly traveled to volunteers at the local animal shelter and a rescue coordinator. They gathered at the house and spent several days hiding in the bushes in order to capture the outdoor cats and transport them to a nearby veterinarian for medical attention. The son reluctantly granted them permission to rescue the four cats left inside the house. Eventually, the shelter and rescue coordinator found homes for all twelve cats, both locally and nationally through the Internet.

Fortunately, this story had a happy ending, but the sad part is that horror stories like this one are all too common, and they usually don't end happily for the pets. If you've ever volunteered at your local animal shelter or subscribed to an Internet email list for pet lovers, you probably have a tragedy or two of your own to tell. The truth is that while many of the dogs, cats, and other pets that end up in animal shelters are surrendered by owners because of an impending move to a home where pets are banned, because allergies have developed in one of the human family members, or because a new baby has arrived on the scene – the three most common excuses for giving up a pet – a significant number of beloved, well-cared-for pets arrive there because the owner suddenly dies or enters a nursing home or other extended-care facility and neglected to make arrangements for the pet's continued care. Or they may have figured a family member or friend would welcome their pet into their home.

That's probably what the man in Long Island thought.

The Meaning Behind PerPETual Care
You may know that the term *perpetual care* is commonly

used in cemeteries, where a person pays a set fee to a cemetery in exchange for regular care and maintenance of the area around the grave, which includes regular mowing and care of the tombstone or grave marker.

In this book, the term PerPETual Care follows along the same lines as it relates to the future of your pet, although it may not necessarily involve money. In essence, PerPETual Care means that you make plans for the continued survival of your pets in the event you are unable to care for them, due to either disability or death. This is usually accomplished by appointing a caretaker and/or providing a sum of money in order to support your pets in the lifestyle and manner to which they are accustomed. Though this may appear to be pretty straightforward, you will soon discover that there are a wide variety of ways to make plans and carry out your wishes for your pets, as well as countless legal loopholes and accounting tasks to take into consideration when choosing your options.

Make Plans *Now*

Various news reports indicated that life insurance salespeople saw an increase in new policies written in the wake of September 11th. Other media stories told of the pets left behind in homes and apartments when their owners lost their lives in the tragedy. And then there were the thousands of cats, dogs, and other pets that were relinquished to shelters near military bases when their owners were called up to active duty and hadn't made plans for their temporary care.

It's a good bet that many of those much-loved pets met their ends in shelters that were overcrowded to begin with. It's the same old story: too many animals, not enough loving homes. How many of these animals would be alive today if their owners had made a few simple arrangements for their caretaking, whether temporary or permanent?

There's a vast array of choices when it comes to your pets' future without you. You'll learn about pet trusts, how to plan for care if you are temporarily incapacitated or disabled, and about the recent phenomenon of pet retirement homes that have begun to pop up all across the country. The chapters that follow describe these options in detail and will provide you with the pros and cons of each. One caution: While one of the choices may immediately make sense to you, it's a good idea to discuss all of the possibilities with a legal or financial-planning professional. In addition, as more states pass laws that legalize the use of pet trusts as an estate-planning tool, it's necessary to learn the specifics of meeting these legal guidelines. After all, what works for your sister in New York may not be applicable for you in New Jersey.

Of course, your own temperament will also influence the choices you make once you learn of all the options that are open to you. While you may love the idea of having your local humane society welcome your pets into their pet retirement program in case something happens to you, other people may prefer that their pets spend their remaining years with friends or family, or in a private home with a new adoptive family.

Your pets have a say in the matter as well. If there's a risk they may have to be separated or move into a home with lots of other animals underfoot when they're used to a quiet home, these considerations will also be factors influencing your decision.

The important thing is to not wait one more day to make plans.

IF YOU THINK YOU'RE ALL SET

Since you've picked up this book, you are obviously concerned about the fate of your pets if you're no longer there to care for them. I know, however, that there's still a small part of you that believes you don't have to make special arrangements for your pet's continued care in the event of your demise. Do any of the following reasons sound familiar?

"I don't have to make plans because I'm sure my family will take the dog." Think again. You may have already asked a family member at the last reunion a few years ago to take care of your pet, and she readily agreed to your request. However, that same relative today may no longer be willing or able to take in a pet. Indeed, she may have even forgotten about her commitment to you or she may have too many pets of her own now.

"I'll definitely outlive my pets." True, you do have a good chance of surviving your pets, especially if they are older, but do you really want to take the chance that the animals you care for and love will end up in a shelter because you failed to take a few steps to ensure that they will live out their natural lives without you? Keep in mind that while the story of the man with the twelve cats had a happy ending, the majority of stories turn out differently. In fact, at least once a week on rescue email lists, a plea for help will appear about the 30 or 40 animals a breeder or rescuer left behind when she unexpectedly died. As her family members are usually too overwhelmed with grief to deal with the animals, complete strangers often have to step in to assist.

"I've written a clause into my will stating that one of my friends has agreed to take the pets, so I'm all set." Not so fast. You've taken an admirable step, and it's more than most pet owners have done, but most of the time a will doesn't get

read until at least several weeks after the flowers from the funeral have wilted. What if no one in your family or immediate circle of friends knows about the plans in your will? And even if your wishes are known, who will care for the animals in the interim before they head for their new home?

It's Easy to Plan PerPETual Care

Whether you choose to appoint a pet caretaker, draw up a pet trust, or make arrangements with a sanctuary or pet retirement home, the actual planning doesn't take much time to complete. While you'll need to know about all of the options that are open to you, as you read through the book and perform some of the planning tasks I suggest, the PerPETual Care plan that will work best for you and your pets will start to become clear.

Take a poll of your pet-owning friends. How many of them have made plans for their own pets in case something happens to them? I'd wager to guess that not many have; after all, while it's hard enough to think of losing a beloved pet, it's even harder to consider your own mortality. As a result, most of us just don't do it. Or if we even think about it, we never seem to get around to it. When dealing with such a sensitive subject, there's safety in numbers, so get a group of friends together – maybe a gathering of volunteers at your local humane society or all the students from the last dog-obedience class you attended – and do the planning together. You may want to gain some perspective by first reviewing the reasons owners gave for surrendering an animal to your local shelter over the last year: What percentage of animals ended up there because the owner got sick, died, or had to enter a nursing home? Depending upon where you live, the results could be eye-opening.

While some shelters will readily divulge this information,

others won't, and you'll have to dig for the statistics in state government documents. A survey conducted between 1994 and 1997 by the National Council on Pet Population Study and Policy (www.petpopulation.org) reported that 64 percent of all pets that entered the participating shelters for any reason were euthanized. State animal control associations tend to report euthanasia statistics as a matter of course, so you can contact them directly. The National Animal Control Association (www.nacanet.org) has links to many state animal control departments. These reports may not include a breakdown of reasons why animals are relinquished, but the sheer numbers of pets that are given up to die each year is sickening.

HOW TO USE THIS BOOK

Although taking the necessary steps to plan for your pets' future may sometimes be difficult emotionally for you (as well as for friends and other family members), it's important that you proceed consistently and thoroughly with the planning. At the same time, try to complete your PerPETual Care plans as quickly as you can in order to protect your pets and provide you with the peace of mind that everything is taken care of when it comes to their welfare. It's not necessary to complete every item in the *What To Do Now* list posted at the end of every chapter before you go on to read the following chapter. In fact, if you can, it's a good idea to read the entire book while you complete the lists in earlier chapters so that you have an idea of the tasks you'll need to accomplish in the future.

Read with a pen in your hand and jot down thoughts and ideas as they occur to you. I've left extra space in the margins so you can do just that. In a few places in the book, I'll ask you to write out detailed plans, so you may want to equip yourself with a notebook that you devote strictly to your PerPETual Care planning. While some readers may prefer to take notes and "think out loud" on a computer, sometimes the act of putting pen to paper can uncover thoughts and ideas that wouldn't have otherwise floated up from your consciousness. And since you're going to be thinking about such an important topic as your pets' future, you'll want to be able to explore all the possibilities that are available to you.

In addition, you should set aside a separate file folder for each one of your pets, to create an individual PerPETual Care kit. You're going to need to gather numerous items, and the kit will ensure you'll be able to keep everything in one place.

Once you're ready to start, either by yourself or with a group of other pet owners, take a deep breath. While you will have numerous options to explore for your pets' own PerPETual Care, it will help immensely if you can keep your sense of humor as you work through the book. Yes, while planning for your pets' future without you is a serious topic, how many times a day do you laugh or smile at something your dog or cat did? If you treat the topic and your planning activities as a total downer, you may find it difficult to carry through with the plan that's best for your pets because, frankly, it will be too depressing. Remember, you owe it to your pets.

Obviously, no one wants to think about their own demise, but if you're like most pet lovers, you'd do anything for your furry friends – even arranging for their PerPETual Care when you haven't taken care of your own, like writing your will. Take this opportunity to begin thinking about writing your own will and making your own final wishes known, after you take care of your pets' future. One good book to get you started is *Prepare Your Own Will: The National Will Kit* by Daniel Sitarz, from Nova Publishing Company. This and other books are listed in the bibliography.

A note about the use of the word *pets* throughout the book. To many pet lovers, animals are like potato chips; few people can have only one. And so I've chosen to favor *pets* over *pet*, and hope that single-pet owners are not offended; rather, a multiple-pet household can be something to aspire to one day.

In addition, I also refer to cats and dogs more often in *PerPETual Care* than to other pets such as horses, birds, ferrets, iguanas, tropical fish, and so on. Please realize that the idea of PerPETual Care should apply to all animals fortunate enough to have the love of a human in their lives. Regardless of the type of pet who has chosen you, it's important to plan for their future whether or not you happen to be around.

What To Do Now

- Begin to consider what would work best for your own peace of mind and your pets' future when it comes to their continued care.
- Gather a group of pet-loving friends to work together on your plans.
- Visit a shelter to see how many well-loved pets were turned in because their owners didn't plan for their futures.
- Think about writing your own will.

2

The Essentials

First of all, you deserve hearty congratulations for taking steps to ensure that your pets will have a future if you're not around, either temporarily or permanently. You should know that you fall into a very small category of people who love their pets enough that they want to make sure the animals will live out their natural lifespans regardless of what the future brings. While the odds are slim that your pets will outlive you, especially if you're young and relatively healthy, they do nonetheless exist.

Of course, blind trust and sheer ignorance have something to do with the fact that more people don't realize the necessity of making PerPETual Care plans: trust in their family and friends' desire to help out and take in pets that have unexpectedly been orphaned; ignorance because they don't realize that if their beloved pets end up in a shelter, their lives will likely end soon after the owner's does.

By picking up this book, you're proving that you care enough about your pets to do the essential work to take care of their futures.

Let's get started.

Eat, Sleep, Crap. Eat, Sleep, Crap.

It's time for "A Day in the Life of Your Pet." Complete with pictures.

In other words, you are going to draw up a complete daily schedule for each pet you want to be covered by a PerPETual Care plan, even if it consists of no more than most cats' and dogs' three most common activities. You will need to include special weekly, monthly, quarterly, and yearly events as well, from grooming to visiting the vet to the Dog Bone of the Month club. Truthfully, the background you provide for each pet will probably be more detailed than the schedule. These details are necessary not only in order to draw up an annual budget for each pet but also to provide a temporary or permanent caretaker with specific information about the care and personality of each pet, along with a health history. Plus, if your cat or dog requires regular medicines or special pet foods, include this information as well. You may want to tear a label off the animal's normal pet food can, box, or bag and include it with the schedule for reference. At this point, it's a good idea to create that separate file folder for each pet, as I mentioned in the last chapter and tuck all the items into this, your PerPETual Care kit, for safekeeping.

To expedite my own planning – I'm creating PerPETual Care kits for my furry kids as I write this book – I'll include real-life examples for one of my twelve cats for you, but you can feel free to include as many or as few details as you like in your schedules and descriptions, whatever you think is necessary.

First, you'll want to write a description of the pet's history and personality, including details about any quirks and feuds or love fests with other animals in your home; see *All About Squatter* on page 15. And if you can convince your vet to give you copies of all medical records for each pet, placing a copy into each pet's file can provide a future caretaker with invaluable information.

Then, write out a typical daily schedule for your pets. It doesn't have to be that detailed, and you may actually have to pad it a bit. See *Squatter's Schedule* for an example. Obviously, in a multi-pet household, much of the information is going to be identical to your other pets' schedules. But that's okay since it means less work for you. You'll want to add weekly outings here, to the groomer and dog park, to agility training, and visits to the vet and anything else that's a part of your regular schedule.

Photos are a must as well. Of course, it's not necessary to take a photo of each pet engaged in each task, but you'll want to include at least one photo in each PerPETual Care kit, especially if you have more than one pet.

The last task is to try to come up with a dollar amount of how much you spend on that particular pet in the course of one year, including food, vet visits, toys, litter, obedience training, kenneling, and so on. Of course, there are discounts in numbers but, for the most part, you'll want to come up with a ballpark figure for each pet. For instance, how much food does Max the mutt consume in one week? If you're having a hard time extrapolating his food intake from all the other animals that scarf up at the same bowl, measure the amount of food you go through with all your pets and then divide by the number of pets. Multiply that amount by 52, and figure on the result as the annual food cost for Max. For example, if you have five dogs who go through a total of twenty pounds of dry food and seven cans of canned food each week, add up the costs to get the total cost for the week, and then multiply it by 52. Then divide by five to get Max's share.

Next, gather up all your vet bills from the last year, a full twelve months. Add them all up and divide by the number of pets; if you have more than one type of pet, separate the charges into categories to come up with the total spent on veterinary care for cats, dogs, horses, birds, rabbits, iguanas, and so on. Divide that figure by the number of that particular kind of pet. The caveat here is that, for the most part, younger and smaller pets will incur smaller veterinary bills than larger and older animals, but not always. Play it safe by tacking at least 25 percent extra onto each animal's annual veterinary bill, and then another 25 percent for any animal over the age of seven.

Proceed in the same way with the other items you spend money on for your pets. You may want to add a couple of details about each pet as they relate to the subject at hand; for instance, if the pet eats more or less or is an absolute addict when it comes to dog biscuits or catnip.

The final figure may turn out to be a big shock if you've never really sat down to figure out exactly how much you spend on your pets each year. It's always good to know where your money goes and it will be a big help later on when you have to figure out how much money you'll need to provide to your pets' new caretakers. See *Squatter's Annual Costs* for how I dealt with it.

ALL ABOUT SQUATTER

Squatter is a neutered male indoor-only cat, probably around 13 years old. I've had him for about seven years. He has hip dysplasia, which causes him to basically march when he walks. As he's gotten older, his back legs have weakened a bit, but he's still able to jump onto counters and manage to clop up and down the stairs.

He does have allergies, and when he starts to wheeze as if he's hacking up a hairball but the wheezing continues for a few days in a row, several times a day, it's time to bring him to the vet for a Depo shot (for his allergies), which works for about six months. For one day about every two weeks, he loses his appetite and curls up in a ball, generally acting sick. Usually, the next day, he's fine. He's a real beggar when it comes to people food, and he'll stop at nothing before he finally gets a few scraps. On those occasions when he's gorged on people food, he acts very quiet for the next 24 hours until he's back to his old self.

His kidneys are in good shape for a cat his age, but his liver has shown some slightly abnormal levels in regular vet tests, so the vet continues to monitor this during regular checkups and Depo visits.

Squatter is a loner kind of guy, and he could easily be an only cat. His nemesis is Beast, though since I've added more cats to the household, her venom tends to be focused elsewhere. He really doesn't like to play like the other cats; he's content to sit by my lap as I work.

SQUATTER'S SCHEDULE:

6 a.m.: Wakes up with the rest of the herd, eats one-quarter of a six-ounce can of cat food before ambling off to find a patch of sun to sleep in for the morning.

Noon: Wakes up to see what I'm having for lunch.

3 p.m.: After I take a shower after my daily run, Squatter jumps in the tub to explore the dripping faucet.

4 p.m.: Starts to hover around me and meow to remind me that it's time for the late-afternoon edition of canned food, also known as wet stink in my house.

4:02 p.m.: Squatter gets his wish.

4:05 p.m.: Wanders off to find a patch of late-afternoon sun to doze in.

7:00 p.m.: Sits at the back door for the evening edition of Kitty TV: in summer, Squatter stares at the birds at the feeder and the moths flinging themselves against the porch light; in winter, he watches the snow fly.

10:00 p.m.: Lights out, Squatter settles in for the night.

Three annual vet visits, twice for Depo, once for a checkup and shots.

SQUATTER'S ANNUAL COSTS

Squatter eats most of the food I put out for all of the other cats, which consists of Wellness dry food and storebrand canned food.

Food: (Annual cost of food for twelve cats):
Two five-pound bags of Wellness food each week at $16 per bag x 52 = $1664 divided by twelve cats = $138.67

Four six-ounce cans store-brand canned cat food (two cans in a.m., two cans in p.m.) = $2/day x 365 = $730 divided by twelve = $60.85. Squatter is one of those cats who eats more of the canned food, so I'll increase his annual cost up to $70 for the year.

Special treats like Pounce or dried sardines, two packages each month for the entire brood, $5 x 12 months = $60 divided by 12 = $5 annually for Squatter.

Squatter's annual food cost: $215 (rounded up)

Vet care:
Checkup and shots once a year: $70 + 25 percent for unknowns ($17.50), plus another 25 percent since he's over the age of seven ($17.50), plus $25 twice a year for Squatter's two Depo shots= $155.00

Grooming:
I don't bring the cats to the groomer, but if you have your pets groomed on a regular basis, be sure to add this cost in as well.

Toys:
$20 (I spend $240 a year on toys and catnip.)

Cat Litter:
I go through three 40-pound bags of brand-name clay litter once a week. Each bag costs about $6 at the local wholesale club store. That's $18 each week, or $1.50 per cat. Multiply that by 52, and Squatter's litter cost is $78 a year. Plus, I replace the litter trays at least once a year, which easily adds $240 a year, or $20 per cat, so his yearly share of the litter cost is $98 per year.

Miscellaneous:
This category can include everything from the gas I spend to get to the vet, money I pay a local girl to feed the cats and change the litter on nights when I'm not home, plus the cost for pumping the septic tank once a year instead of every three years. I'll put Squatter's share at $50.

In this category, you'll want to include the cost of repairs to scratched furniture and cleaning the rugs and other general household maintenance due to the pets, as well as any other related costs you can think of.

Therefore, Squatter's total is $538 a year, although this figure could easily double with one emergency visit to the vet, plus an overnight stay, medication, lab tests, return visits, and other expenses.

In Case of Emergency

If you do nothing else suggested in this book, you'll need to create notices in the form of wallet cards and signs to hang in your home that will inform emergency workers of the existence of your pets and what to do about them in case something happens to you or a disaster occurs in your town or at your home. A wallet card should contain the names and phone numbers of the people who have agreed to step in and care for your pets in case you are not able to; you'll decide on these names later. You can also tuck a wallet card inside the glove compartment of each car that you drive on a regular basis, and give each of your chosen caregivers a copy; if your first choice cannot care for your pets, she should know who her alternate is. See my example of a wallet card on page 20.

It's also important to create a sign that includes not only the names and phone numbers of your pets' foster parents or temporary caregivers, but also the number of pets that currently live in your home so that police and firefighters know how many to save. Hang the sign in several places in your home: on your refrigerator, on the inside of all doors that lead out of the house, and on the wall of a garage, barn, or other outbuilding. The sign doesn't have to be fancy; it's a good idea to use red ink to print it out so that strangers in your house won't miss it. See my example.

If Disaster Strikes

In addition to the tales of people who died on September 11th leaving pets behind, a common story that surfaced in the wake of the disaster told of the number of pets that were left alone for days in apartments without food and water all over the New York metropolitan area. Entire sections of the city were shut down, electricity and water were shut off, and people could not rescue their stranded pets for days, in some

Sample Wallet Card

IN CASE OF EMERGENCY

I have 12 cats located at 212 Kinsman Road in Grafton, New Hampshire, that will need immediate care if I am injured or killed.

Please contact Karen Meyers and Richard Blair, at 603-523-5555; they have agreed to assume temporary responsibility for their care.

Sample Emergency Sign for House

IN CASE OF EMERGENCY

There are 12 cats located in this house. Since some are afraid of strangers, you'll have to look in all of the closets and in any place that may seem like a good place to hide.

For help, you can call Karen Meyers or Richard Blair at 603-523-5555.

Cat carriers are located in the barn.

cases. In fact, Animal Planet's *Animal Precinct* show about the ASPCA devoted an entire show to the rescue efforts that were made.

In many cases, the temporary-care options you've already read about can also apply to your situation if a disaster should strike, like a hurricane or tornado, flood or fire. Disaster planning experts recommend that you assemble a Pet Disaster Kit. The United Animal Nations' Emergency Rescue Service has lots of good information at its website: www.uan.org. Here's what they recommend for each pet:

- A one-week supply of food and water.
- A one-week supply of medication complete with copies of all medical records and vaccination records; the latter are especially important since they are required in order to board a pet at most kennels or for air transport.
- A one-week supply of cat litter and a collapsible or disposable litter box; pooper scooper and sufficient scooper bags for dogs.
- A collapsible cage or carrier for each animal. Many emergency workers recommend the Evacsak for cats, which are pillow-shaped and somewhat waterproof; see www.animal-care.com for details.
- A pet first aid kit, which you can purchase at pet shops or online at www.medipet.com.
- Blankets or a pet bed.
- A collar and tag with the pet's name, your vet's phone number, and your cell phone number, even if your pet does not normally wear one.
- A copy of your pet's schedule, which also lists your veterinarian's name.

- Miscellaneous items, including a flashlight and fresh batteries, paper towels and disinfectant, and a couple of favorite toys.
- Place each kit within easy access of the front door of your home.

Line up a nearby kennel or boarding facility in advance; most shelters set up by the Red Cross during natural disasters prohibit people from bringing their pets along so you'll need to board your pets until you can return home.

If a disaster does strike and you need to evacuate your home, make sure you round up your pets when you first leave home. Emergency workers will probably prohibit you from entering your home after a flood or tornado to rescue your pets due to the obvious danger a damaged house presents; that is, if the animals are still in the house. By the time authorities deem it safe to return, it may be too late.

A Change in Plans

One important thing to realize as you proceed with your planning is that the documents you draw up will probably tend to change and need to be updated over time. Even with the schedules you just created, your pets do change with each passing year, just like people. If a cat becomes diabetic six months after you drew up the schedule, obviously this expense and the once- or twice-daily task that go along with it will need to be added both to your pet's schedule and your budget. In addition, you may acquire new pets and old ones may die. You'll need to update your records with each change in your household.

As you continue to plan in later chapters, and appoint friends, family members, and possibly legal and financial professionals to help carry out your PerPETual Care plans, keep in mind that these individuals will also undoubtedly change. Some may move away, others may lose interest, and still others may die or become incapacitated themselves. This is the first time – but not the last – that I'll tell you that nothing is permanent when it comes to your PerPETual Care plans. You'll need to check in with all of the details and people involved in each pet's plan at least once a year, and preferably twice. Reviewing each plan will take very little time, but it's better to be safe than sorry when the stakes involve your pets' futures.

PLANS A, B, AND C

At the present time, I have 12 cats and my boyfriend has 8; that's 20 felines in all between two houses. We've always had an unspoken agreement that if something happened to either of us, the other one would inherit the other's cats, despite the fact that 20 cats in either house would be a bit crowded, but no matter, that's what we'd do.

After I learned about the horror stories of the pets left behind in the case of an owner's illness or death and began to research this book, one thing began to nag at me. What if something happened to both of us at the same time? What would become of all 20 cats? I discovered that it was necessary to have a variety of plans for our cats' PerPETual Care due to life's unpredictability. And of course, due to the 20 cats between us, it was obvious that we couldn't count on the kindness of friends *or* strangers.

As I began to draw up my own plans for my cats' lives without me, we did the same thing for all 20 cats if they were suddenly left without two humans to care for them. This presented a big problem. In the rural towns where we live, most people let their cats outside at least part of the time, and all of our 20 cats were strictly indoor felines. As a result, we couldn't turn to our friends to accept even a few, since the cats that arrived in our lives already declawed would be totally defenseless once outside. Our thinking obviously had to get a bit creative.

As does yours. These are the exact things you have to consider and the kinds of questions you'll need to ask yourself in the pages to come.

What To Do Now

- Create a PerPETual Care kit for each of your pets.
- Draw up a schedule for each of your pets, complete with details and personality quirks.
- Calculate your annual expenses for each pet, including food, vet bills, toys, litter, and miscellaneous items.
- Create a wallet card and sign to alert emergency workers to the pets in your home.
- Assemble a pet disaster kit for each pet.
- Expect aspects of your plan to change.
- Develop a Plan A, B, and C.

3

Finding Your PerPETual Caretaker

As you've already discovered, making sure that your pets are cared for if you are not able to is probably more complex than you had imagined. The same goes for finding a person or organization willing to assume full responsibility for the caretaking of your pets.

Though you may already have someone in mind – and indeed, may have already asked that someone to serve – it's not as simple as asking your sister or best friend and having them give you their verbal okay. You'll need to get it all down in writing, have it notarized and filed with your legal papers, and arrange for an alternate who will step in if your first choice is not able to.

There's also the issue of money to consider. Your best friend may refuse any monetary compensation in exchange for taking your pets into his home; indeed, money may never come up as an issue. As you've discovered in Chapter Two, raising one pet – let alone ten – is not an inexpensive proposition. You want to be fair, so show him the budgets you've worked out for each pet. However, if he still refuses your financial support, you can show your appreciation by denoting that a treasured keepsake of yours will be left to him in your will.

Find an Adopter, Temporary or Permanent

If you can line up a friend or family member to agree to take in your pets in case something should happen to you, then you're pretty lucky.

If you already have this all taken care of, you may think you don't need to read the rest of the book, but stay with me, because there's a lot of important information to come, from arranging for the financial care of your pets to drawing up formal agreements and contracts so the new owner will have no questions about caring for your pets.

However, if you're like most pet owners, you may find you have a hard time finding a friend or relative to accept one or all of your pets into their homes and who may give you a raft of lame excuses about why they can't possibly do it. If you can't find someone to agree to your requests, don't worry. You'll discover a variety of alternatives for your pets in later chapters. You may, however, find you can convince these same people to act as temporary foster parents. Choose a minimum of two individuals who will agree to take care of your pets in the days that immediately follow an accident or death. In the aftermath of such a crisis, it's sometimes easy for others to neglect your pets, and this interim period is the most likely time that an unsuspecting person will come along and drop them off at the shelter, where their future will be far from secure.

You'll probably need to provide some funds to the foster parents to help pay for your pets' care. There are several ways you can accomplish this. One is to set up a separate interest-bearing checking account that is held in trust in case it's needed; an attorney or the bank manager can help you to make these arrangements. Another option is to write a check for a specified amount made out to the foster parent. Don't date the check, keep it in a safe place in your home, and make sure the foster parent knows where it is. Refer back to your budget and allow for one to two months worth of expenses for each pet: "a few days" can easily turn into several months when the law is involved or you're recovering from a temporary setback.

You should make it clear to the foster parent that this temporary situation may indeed last for a couple of months, until your will is read or your estate enters probate and the transfer of permanent ownership occurs, or until you get back on your feet and are able to assume responsibility for your pets again. You should give the foster parent a copy of each pet's schedule and background information along with the keys to your house and written instructions on where they can find the pet food, medication, and pet carriers. Once you select a permanent home for your pets, you can add this information to your PerPETual Care kit.

WHO TO ASK

Obviously, you'll need to consider people who are bona fide pet lovers – at least lovers of your type of pet – and then realistically consider if it's possible for them to take in any more pets. You can dismiss certain candidates without even approaching them due to their living situations; for instance, one friend may love animals but live in a studio apartment with several dogs and already be at her limit. Another may live on a country estate and have lots of room for animals of all kinds, but her cats and dogs live in the main house and freely go outside through a pet access door – your cats are declawed and must remain strictly house cats. And so on.

Depending upon the number and type of pets you have, you may have to split them up between friends and relatives. On the other hand, you may choose to stipulate that your pets must stay together. However, if you find one person who readily agrees to take one of your pets into their home but none of the others, seriously consider the offer, especially if you are falling short of eager pet caretakers within your circle of friends and family – and especially if there's any danger of a pet ending up in a shelter, where chances for a long and healthy life for your pets are radically diminished.

On a side note: When a shelter stipulated that a certain pair of cats had to be adopted out together, I've adopted cats in pairs. True, they may have been glued to each other in the shelter, but that was probably more out of fear than their deep love for one other. Once I got them home and settled in, I would swear that the inseparable pair never once gave each other the time of day, as far as I could tell.

Whoever you choose as a pet caretaker, the important thing to keep in mind is that if someone rejects the idea out of hand – despite being a pet lover – do not force the issue even if this person is the top candidate on your list. After all, you wouldn't want to leave your pets with someone who was less than enthusiastic about the idea. Taking in the pets of a close friend or relative is a big responsibility (and often a lot of work) and you shouldn't take your selection of pet caretaker lightly.

You'll also want the future guardian of your beloved pets to be trustworthy – being an animal lover is not enough. Does this person have enough of a routine that she'll be able to walk your dogs at regular intervals? Is she settled enough in her life to be able to provide the stability all pets crave? Is there any chance that she may drop everything and move across the country for her dream job and take her pets with her, but not yours?

Above all, it's important to ask, and not leave it to chance. You may smile at the thought of your favorite nephew's pleasure upon hearing the news that you've left him your classic Mustang convertible that he's always loved, but most people would not be thrilled to discover that you've left them property in the form of living, breathing animals, and neglected to tell them when you had the chance. Trust me: Even if they've paid a lot of attention to your pets in the past, and loved to take them out for long walks, they'll want to know about their new status as pet foster parent first. After all, they may not be living the same lifestyle if the time should come for your wishes to be carried out.

The person you choose should be aware that your pets will undoubtedly be traumatized by your sudden absence and also by being uprooted from familiar surroundings and placed in a new home with strange noises, smells, people, and pets. Ideally, your caretaker will be sensitive to your pets' fears and apprehensions and provide them with plenty of time, space, and attention to get acclimated. If she has taken in abandoned or orphaned pets in the past, so much the better.

If you're in the position of having too many people to choose from, you should consider yourself fortunate. Here, it may help to put yourself in the mindset of each of your pets. If it were up to your pet to decide who should serve as his guardian, who would he choose? In asking this question for each pet, you may have to split them up for their own well-being. Be honest. If you "hear" a clear answer from each pet about their desired guardian, when it comes time to break the news to the guardian, you can truthfully say to your sister or neighbor, "Mickey picked you!"

By the way, this is not the only time in the book you'll need to get inside your pets' head to continue working on your PerPETual Care kit; in Chapter 8, you'll actually get the opportunity to write a will for each of your pets!

Get It in Writing

Granted, some people still do business on a handshake, but when it comes to the future welfare of your pets, you'll need to get it all down in writing and properly notarized. Afterwards, provide everyone involved with copies of the details, from your lawyer and veterinarian to family members and your desired caretaker.

Although you'll learn about proper legal language and trusts and wills in later chapters, you should know that it is possible to draw up a valid legal document that is as brief as one sentence in length. Again, keep in mind that since pets are considered to be property in the eyes of the law, using words like "custody" and "bequest" may actually result in invalidating your wishes and endangering the lives of your pets. The minimum you'd need to be recognized by law is: "I leave my cats Huey, Louie, and Dewey, and my dogs, Riff and Raff, to my daughter, Marilyn."

The problem is that if this sentence exists only within the context of a will and you've made no interim care arrangements, your pets' lives could be in jeopardy, unless you've named Marilyn on your emergency wallet card and house signs. Plus, you'll need to provide Marilyn with copies of your PerPETual Care kits for all of your pets along with your named alternate caregiver in case Marilyn is not able to assume responsibility.

THE LONG ARM OF THE LAW

Since the law considers pets to be property, and pets obviously cannot make decisions on their own, you may need to grant a durable power of attorney to a close friend or relative who can make important decisions for your pets if you cannot. This can be the same person you appoint as foster parent or your chosen permanent caregiver. The important thing to keep in mind is that this person needs to take immediate action for the welfare of your pets, with free access to your home and pets.

A power of attorney grants the person you specify the authority to take charge of your personal affairs while you are alive but unable to make decisions under your own power due to physical or mental illness. A power of attorney is considered to be a temporary measure, in place until more permanent arrangements can take effect. It's important to understand that while a person who is granted power of attorney wields considerable power to meet your wishes concerning the care of your pets, it doesn't necessarily mean that he will be as conscientious as you when it comes to their daily care. For this reason, it's a good idea to select a fellow animal lover to have temporary jurisdiction over your affairs, since this way it's a pretty good bet that your pets will receive the care and attention they're used to, or close to it.

To streamline things, it may be a good idea to grant power of attorney to the same people you choose to be your replacement as pet parents, although some planning experts suggest that you give the power of attorney and temporary caretaker to two separate individuals in order to put a series of checks and balances into place concerning the care of your pets. You should know this is not the only time I'll suggest appointing two people to carry out different aspects of one PerPETual Care arrangement. In many instances, it's an important principal to help insure the security of your pets.

On this last point, whatever you choose to do by the end of the book, it's a good idea to have a lawyer review the documents you draw up; that is, if you choose to draft these legal papers yourself. (See Appendix B for a list of pet-friendly lawyers throughout the country.)

After all, if a relative chooses to contest the arrangements you've made for your beloved pets – it wouldn't be the first time – you've already had it vetted by at least one attorney who would be able to point out any potential loopholes and red flags to you.

SHELTERS AS CARETAKERS

It may not be the first choice that comes to mind, but you may want to consider appointing your favorite animal shelter or humane society to serve as the primary guardian for your pets, on either a temporary or permanent basis. Many shelters and humane organizations have permanent-care arrangements with their members. In exchange for a donation, the shelter will agree to take care of your pets for the remainder of their natural lifespan. This care can occur in the shelter itself, although numerous shelters across the country have designated or even bought or constructed specific buildings to serve as housing for pets they've accepted into their long-term care program.

Other shelters will agree to take in your pets in exchange for a donation and keep them until they are adopted. In one California shelter, these pets have do-not-euthanize tags on their cages, but then again, especially if your pets are older, the chances for adoption are low. Do you really want your beloved animals to spend the rest of their lives in a cage? Plus, you may want to have a bit more say about the adoptive home rather than leaving the decision to a volunteer with discretion to place pets with anyone who walks through the door. The time to exert your influence is before it's necessary, not later when you're not around.

It goes without saying that you should familiarize yourself with the routines of the shelter and determine if its degree of care for your pets matches your own. If you direct the shelter to find a home for your pets, research their adoption policies and make any requests in advance. Keep in mind that more than a few general requests about a future home for your pets may render them unadoptable; after all, who else could meet your high standards when it comes to your furry family members?

As it turns out, many shelters and humane organizations appear to be very open to creating a plan that works for you, especially if you've been a long-standing member and have donated regularly. One man with a pot-bellied pig arranged for the director of his local humane organization to take his pet when he dies. He opened a savings account with his name and the director's name on it, and the money in the account will support not only the pig's expenses but will serve as an additional last donation from him as well. If you have some ideas about how your shelter can benefit along with your pets, make an appointment with the shelter director or the person in charge of managing bequests and donations. You should be able to come up with a plan that makes everyone happy.

There's more information about how shelters and other facilities provide PerPETual Care in Chapter Seven.

THE BEST-LAID PLANS...HAVING A BACKUP

Despite the fact that your chosen caretaker has lived in the same town and house all his life, has held the same job for 30 years, and has raised a series of happy-go-lucky dogs and content cats through their entire lifespans, life does have a nasty tendency of getting in the way every so often.

For this reason, it's important that you have a backup plan in case your chosen guardian is not able to take responsibility for your pets. Or perhaps you feel comfortable enough with his animal talent and judgment to allow him to choose the next home for your pets if he can't follow through. You may in fact decide to choose more than one caretaker to serve as your backup.

Use the same criteria in selecting an alternate caregiver as you did when choosing your primary guardian. Discuss it openly with your prospects, listen to what your pets tell you, and then be sure you provide all of the people involved with all the information they need in order to give your pets the full, happy life they deserve.

A Few More Options

Another option you may choose is to assign your caretaker the freedom to adopt out your pets to new homes, with the caveat that there be no hurry to place them. A safe, loving home is the most important issue. In essence, then, the guardian takes on a quasi-temporary status; this would work particularly well if she is active in the community or participates at the local humane organization.

Some pet owners have appointed the executor of their entire estate to serve as the primary individual responsible for choosing between at least two potential guardians, as named by the owner. Though this option may initially seem unfair to the executor, it will save you as pet owner the trouble of perennially checking with each of your choices to see if they're still committed to taking in your pets if something should happen to you. You can direct the executor to assess the environment and living situations at each home, and then use his judgment to select the best home for each of your pets. After all, though your favorite caretaker may have agreed to accept all your pets, by the time that action needs to be taken, she may have taken in additional pets, some of which may not get along well with your pets for one reason or another.

If you decide to opt for a trust fund for your pets, you can name the administrator of the trust to bear responsibility for finding a new adoptive home for your pets. The advantage here is that the trustee signs the checks for expenses disbursed from the trust and, in interviewing potential adopters, he can gauge the care and home environment on a firsthand basis and occasionally pay personal visits to the adoptive home to check up on your pets' new home. You'll learn more about trusts in Chapter Six.

What To Do Now

- Be open to assigning your pets to different caretakers, if necessary.
- Make sure you get an agreement in writing with your chosen caretaker.
- Grant a durable power of attorney to a trustworthy friend or relative
- Think about appointing your local shelter to serve as caretaker for your pets.
- Have one or more backups in case your primary caretaker can't follow through.
- Decide whether you want your caretaker to contemplate finding a good home for your pets or whether you would rather have the pets live only with the guardian.

4

Estate Planning
for Pets

The idea of drawing up your own estate plan may have never previously crossed your mind. Now that you're working on your PerPETual Care plan, however, you'll need to start thinking about how to provide the financial means to ensure that your pets live in the style they are accustomed to, or at least close to it.

You may not have to be concerned with figuring out where the money will come from for your pets' future support if a friend or relative has agreed to take them in, no strings attached, and insists on taking no money from you or your estate. If you're in that category, you can take a deep breath and relax...but you can also view this opportunity as the chance to get to work on your own estate-planning issues, which means you can leave some of your money to your favorite animal welfare group.

If you don't have any assets to speak of, you may feel that you can skip over this chapter. Before you turn the page, however, at least read the next section.

What If You Have No Estate?

If you're among the millions of pet owners who spend every spare dollar on your pets, whether your own or whether you're taking in fosters or transporting rescued animals from a kill shelter to their new homes, you can still make arrangements to provide for the financial well-being of your animals. Many people who dedicate themselves to saving animals dream of having their work continue long after they're gone. One way to accomplish this, if you're perennially short on cash, is to take out a life insurance policy that will provide your pets as well as your favorite nonprofit organization with the funds to carry on your work well into the future. Essentially, you can take care of everything by naming your selected caretaker as the primary beneficiary of the policy.

Of course, there are stipulations for being accepted into a particular life insurance program and you have to meet certain health conditions. However, if you lack a significant estate and still want to plan for your pets' future, as well as provide your favorite animal-welfare organizations with an always-needed financial shot in the arm, take out an insurance policy.

If you choose this route, you'll still need to plan your estate – since it will be fully funded upon your death – so I hope you will continue to read.

Finding Pet-Savvy Estate-Planning Experts

Essentially, estate planning will involve at least two professionals: a certified public accountant and an attorney. First of all, you'll want to choose professionals who specialize in trust and estate issues, since attorneys and accountants who have experience drawing up estates and trusts specifically provide for pets are still relatively few and far between. A list of pet-friendly estate-planning lawyers is located in Appendix B. It appears that few accountants and financial planners focus their practice on helping animal lovers to plan for Per-PETual Care; indeed, it appears to be a great growth industry. Perhaps by the time the next edition of this book comes out, I will be able to add a section on pet-friendly CPAs.

Another way to find a qualified professional is to ask your pet-loving friends and family members as well as the staff at your local humane society for referrals. Frequently, shelters and nonprofit animal agencies have attorneys, accountants, and financial planners who consult with them on a pro bono basis and perform legal work and number crunching in the event that a member wants to leave all or part of his estate to the society. If the details haven't been ironed out by the member through a trust or planned annuity, the professionals will help the shelter determine the best way to invest or spend the money to get the best return on the gift. Some professionals market their services to members and offer to work with a client at no charge if the client wants to leave part or all of an estate to the shelter. The lawyers and accountants who do this consider it to be their long-term contribution to a shelter's well-being.

Since these professionals have experience and empathy for animal issues, you'd be wise to consider them for your own estate planning, both for your pet and for your family. After all, the last thing you want is an attorney or accountant who bursts out laughing when you mention that you want to provide for your pets after you're gone.

Ideally, the lawyer and accountant you choose should

have had experience not only working with pet trusts and estate planning but should also have previously worked with each other on such cases. Ask the attorney you contact for the name of an accountant with pet experience, or vice versa. Again, since this is a pretty specialized field at this time, this may be a tall order to fill, although this scenario would be optimal for you and your pets.

Getting Started

For your initial meeting, these professionals will ask you to bring along specific financial and legal records. You'll probably need to gather up all your financial records as well as those of your family members with whom you jointly own assets. Include past tax returns, bank statements, and details and amounts of all of your investments, both liquid and illiquid, from stocks and bonds to real estate and automobiles. You'll also need to have some idea of who you'd like to care for your pets as well as how much money is required to support each pet each year. Be sure to complete as much of your PerPETual Care kits as you can before you pick up the phone to make an appointment with a CPA or lawyer.

Obviously, you'll also need to have some idea of how you want the remainder of your estate to be divided among the humans. You'll need to draw up some plans of how you'd like to leave money to family members that will help them to achieve their goals.

The accountant will help you envision a variety of scenarios on how to divvy up your estate so that it will accomplish the goals of keeping your pets safe and alive as well as your family and friends content. Of course, some of the people you see who drive around in RVs with license plates that say "I'm Spending My Children's Inheritance" may have reserved just enough to set up a trust for their other children –

their pets. Your accountant will also inform you of the tax advantages and disadvantages of your plans, since leaving a lump-sum payout to your pet may mean that half is chewed up in taxes in the first year alone, while choosing a stock-based annuity fund or trust will provide sufficient income each year without that miserable tax bite.

WILLS VS. TRUSTS

One of the most common questions when it comes to estate planning of any kind is, "Do I need a will or a trust, or both?"

The answer is, it depends. The good news is that there are many different ways to construct and write a will or trust. You can pick one – or both – and then refine them according to your own needs. I've devoted an entire chapter to each, to allow for more detail, but here is the difference in a nutshell.

A will spells out how you plan to distribute your estate upon your death, which includes everything that you own, including financial investments and cash and material possessions. A trust essentially administers money from a specific trust account on a predetermined, often periodic, basis to allow for the support of an individual, family, or organization.

The basic difference between them is that the tenets of a will kick in only upon the person's death, and there can be a lengthy delay before the estate is distributed if the will is required to go through probate court in order to determine the validity of the document and to address any challenges. A trust can be activated either in the event of your death or temporary disability and is rarely contested by family, friends, or other beneficiaries. If you've spelled out the terms of care for your pets after your death only in your will and it gets stuck in probate court because of feuding relatives, the lives of your pets will be in real jeopardy unless you've made short-term arrangements with a temporary caretaker.

Many people will only require a will to satisfactorily plan for their pets' future as long as interim care is planned and all those involved are given a copy of the will before death. Other people will need both a will and a trust due to the complexity of an estate while still other pet owners will spell out their plans for their pets' care in a separate trust account while leaving their will devoted strictly to people-oriented issues.

No Surprises

By and large, most people in our culture don't like to talk about money or death. Stories about spouses and relatives who didn't know about the deceased's penchant for a secret pastime until the reading of the will are rampant. Accountants and lawyers have seen the shock and surprise on the faces of family members countless times.

Though your family undoubtedly knows of your love for animals, if you plan to leave part of your estate to support your pets after you're gone but neglect to inform your family about your intentions, you can expect a massive fight to break out among your family members as well as challenges to your estate. As a result, your pets' future could be at stake. Vengeful relatives could charge that you were mentally unstable when you were devising your estate plans and writing your will. Make sure that you break down your estate into percentages that make sense and are not way out of line. Even if you prepare your documents yourself, as I've said before, it's a good idea to have a lawyer review them to check for any possible red flags. For instance, if you expect your estate to total one million dollars – including all of your tangible assets as well as real estate and life insurance pay-outs – you may want to allot 10 percent of this to a trust for the continued care of your pets. The remaining 90 percent could then be divided between family members, nonprofit organizations, and other beneficiaries without anyone complaining that you allotted too much of your estate to your pets.

By doing this, you're deliberately limiting future challenges to your estate. If you were to designate 50 percent or more to your pets, other beneficiaries could view that as grounds for a challenge. There have been instances of people with large estates and few or no relatives or friends who want to leave their entire estate to their pets. In these cases, legal and financial professionals tend to advise against this intention and instead try to help the person locate charities where many more animals could benefit from the money.

Whatever your plans, it's vital that you tell the people in your life what you intend to do to help support your pets in case something happens to you. If you feel that there's any risk of a beneficiary challenging your estate, you'll need to take steps to back up your decisions. Have your attorney or accountant videotape a question-and-answer session with you regarding your desire to care for your pets where you clearly and rationally reiterate the specifics in your estate plan for the distribution of funds and property. And to prevent challenges derived from the accusation that you were not in your right mind when you planned your estate, you may need to solicit notarized statements from doctors, psychologists, and other medical and mental professionals who know you well and will vouch for your state of mind before, during, and after your estate planning.

WHAT TO DO NOW
- If you have no estate, investigate life insurance programs that would fund your PerPETual Care plans.

43

- Find a lawyer and certified public accountant to assist you in planning for your pets.
- Gather together your financial and legal records to help you to decide how much to leave for the support of your pets.
- Learn about the difference between a will and a trust.
- Tell the people in your life what you're planning to do to ensure that your pets are taken care of upon your death.

5

Of Hound Mind
And Body:
Naming Pets in Your Will

Y ou've probably heard news stories about a famous
person dying and in her will leaving everything to
her pets to allow them to carry on in the style
they're accustomed to living: cat food in crystal bowls and
weekly chauffeured trips to the dog groomer. These stories
first began to surface decades ago as believe-it-or-not stories
in gossip columns as a way to poke fun at pet lovers in an era
built largely on restraint. A cat existed solely to catch mice
while a dog's purpose was to guard the house, and that was
the most people expected of their pets back then.

How times have changed. Not only are celebrity leave-it-
all-to-the-pet stories relatively commonplace today – and

people don't laugh, at least not as loudly – but the idea of naming a pet in a Last Will and Testament has caught on among the commonfolk as well. According to one study, between 12 and 27 percent of pet owners in the United States have detailed their pets' future care in their wills. Another report estimates that more than 1 million dogs have been listed in Americans' wills that have gone through probate since 1991. Who knows how high that figure will be in ten years!

Of course, celebrities who want to leave part or all of their estate to their pets today have a posse of financial and legal advisors to help them with their planning. But I'd bet that even they'd be surprised to discover that much more than a will is necessary in order to safeguard their beloved animals.

Why a Will Is Not Enough

As briefly noted in Chapter Four, a will is a good starting point when planning your estate to include the continued care of your pets. Although a will technically is supposed to take effect immediately upon your death, this is not how things usually work out. The delay that can occur between the time of death and the time the will is either read by a lawyer in the presence of beneficiaries and/or is acknowledged by a judge can mean the difference between life and death for your pets, if a will is the only PerPETual Care tool you choose to use. In addition, should a family member or friend – or worse, the guardian you assign as your pets' permanent caretaker – decide to dispute part of the will, your pets could be left in a legal purgatory until the disagreement is settled.

But there's a bigger problem. When you write a will, you detail the kinds of property you are leaving to the loved ones in your life. As a pet owner, your particular dilemma is that, in the eyes of the law, your furry family members are considered to be your personal property and not living, breathing creatures that you can leave material items or financial support to. In other words, the law will regard the clause in your will where you bequeath money or property to your pets after death as the equivalent of leaving your car to your washing machine. However, if you include a clause appointing a human with the responsibility of caring for your pets, along with spelling out the financial support you'll provide from your estate, no red flag will tempt the courts.

If you're particularly stubborn about doing things your own way and include a clause in your will where you leave all or part of your estate to your pets, be forewarned that the law will still get its way. In this case, the estate you "left" to your pets will instead be awarded to one of the beneficiaries you named to receive your personal property, or to your residuary beneficiary, the person frequently named at the end of a will who inherit all of your property that was not specifically named in the will. This will probably be the case even in a pet-friendly state that otherwise recognizes pet trusts. And if you neglect to include your PerPETual Care plans in your will, the courts will likely award your pets to your "next of kin," however that is interpreted.

PLANNING FOR INTERIM CARE: A MUST

You've already learned about arranging for temporary PerPETual Care in the event that you become sick or temporarily out of commission due to a natural or manmade disaster, but it's vital to arrange for interim care if you decide to rely on a will to convey your wishes about the care of your pet after you die.

You now realize that although the bequests in your will

47

take effect immediately upon your death, it can take some time until the court issues documents known as *letters testamentary*, which grant the authority to the executor of your will to proceed in fulfilling the wishes you've detailed in the document. Until the executor is able to proceed, his hands are tied, which is why it's important to assign a person to serve as interim caretaker.

The interim caretaker can be anyone you specify, from a friend or neighbor to executor to the person who will eventually be appointed as your pets' permanent caretaker. However, that temporary care can also be provided by a shelter or the pet professionals you deal with regularly: your veterinarian, groomer, pet sitter, or anyone else. As is the case with permanent care, you'll want to provide a sum of money that will cover your pets' expenses during this time. It's a good idea to think of this budget in terms of weeks, since it's usually unclear how long it will be until the court validates your will.

As is the case with all the people who will be responsible for some facet of your pets' care if something happens to you, make sure they all have copies of the PerPETual Care kits for each pet that will come under their care, even for a brief period of time.

CHOOSE YOUR EXECUTOR WISELY

The person you choose to be the executor of your will is charged with the responsibility of making sure that your wishes are carried out and your estate is gathered together and distributed to the beneficiaries you've named. Sounds simple, and you may already have an obvious choice in mind, but again, where people and pets are involved, you want to be absolutely sure that the person you select will never have less than 100 percent of your pets' best interests at heart. As this person may not necessarily be the same individual you choose to be your pets' permanent caretaker, the executor will need to make sure that your caretaker is working to the letter of the law in the care of your pets. As previously discussed, some people deliberately name two different people – one as executor and one as caretaker – in order to have a series of checks and balances in place, so that one person is not responsible for everything, which may be too much for some people to handle.

Even if you choose the perfect person to be your executor, specificity is a must. If there is any aspect of the pet care clause in your will that is not perfectly clear to everyone, the chance remains that your pets may not be able to live the remainder of their lives as you had intended. For instance, the executor may feel that your choice as permanent guardian is not best for your pets, and she may sabotage the transfer of ownership despite your wishes. Or your designated permanent caretaker may confess to the executor that she'll take in the pets if she has to, but she doesn't have the room and her husband doesn't want any more animals and she only told you she'd take them because she felt sorry for you, and, well, you get the idea.

Your executor is then charged with the task of finding another suitable long-term home for your pets or taking them into her own home. That's why you'll want an executor who is a real animal lover who puts the interest of your pets first because she knows this is what you would have wanted for them. She would expect the same of you if she chose you to be the executor of her estate.

Of course, you'll want your executor to be able to put as much care into fulfilling the other wishes in your will, so having a good sense of business and finance helps as well. In addition, your executor will need to be over 18 and a legal resident of the state you lived in as well as a legal resident of the United States. Some people choose two individuals to serve as co-executors, but most legal experts believe that it's best to have one executor and choose an alternate executor in case your first choice is unable to carry out her duties.

SOME SAMPLE WILL CLAUSES

Wills are simple both by design and in language. They're straightforward legal documents that tell it like it is in as few words as possible. Adjectives are almost strangely nonexistent.

Here are several clauses that run the gamut of possibilities, one of which may be yours.

Plain & Simple: I leave my cat, Spot, and my dog, Tiger, to Robert Wilson, plus any other animals that I own at the time of my death. If Robert is not able to take in my animals, either at the time of my death or at some point in the future, my Executor will choose a suitable person to become their permanent caretaker. I would like my Executor to not separate the animals, if at all possible.

Plan B: I direct my Executor to give my cat, Spot, and my dog, Tiger, to one or more of the following people:

Robert Wilson, presently residing at 100 Main Street, Springfield, New York.

Jane Smith, presently residing at 102 Main Street, Springfield, New York.

David Jones, presently residing at 104 Main Street, Springfield, New York.

I direct my Executor to determine which of the people named above should be given one or both of my pets. If my

Executor believes that none are capable of or willing to give my pets the care and attention I would like, my Executor shall find a suitable caretaker that meets with his discretion.

I direct my Executor to give $1,000 a year for each animal to the person(s) to provide care for them.

Shelter Case: *Upon my death, I give all animals in my possession at that time to the Springfield Humane Society, presently located at 106 Main Street, Springfield, New York, and I make the following requests:*

The Society is to attempt to adopt out the pets – either together or separately – to good, stable, loving homes by people who have already successfully adopted pets from the Society;

If the Society is unable to find suitable homes for one or all of my pets, they are to house them on the shelter premises, uncaged, and sequestered from new intakes and animals under veterinary care;

The Society is to provide them with adequate premium food and regular veterinary checkups. Should any of my pets under their care become ill, regular veterinary care will be administered. Should any of my pets become terminally ill, I request that no heroic measures shall be taken to keep them alive.

And here's a clause to cover interim care of your pets:

After my death, my cat, Spot, and my dog, Tiger, shall be given to Cheryl Smith for the purpose of interim care. The

Executor shall give Cheryl Smith the sum of forty dollars from my estate for each week that these animals are under her care; however, the Executor has the discretion to increase the amount of money should the animals require specialized or veterinary care.

Conduct a Yearly Review

As you keep the documents and items in each of your pets' PerPETual Care kits up to date, you'll also want to periodically review the specific pet care clause in your will. Yes, it will involve some expense to have your attorney update the information – or at least review it for validity and to counter any items that may present conflicts in the future – but it will be worth it in order to avoid any future confusion about your intent and takes into account any change in your beneficiaries' lifestyles or housing situations. If there are many changes – for instance, your primary caretaker has moved away and you've acquired four new pets since you wrote your first will – then it's in your best interest to prepare a completely new will. If there are only a few changes, you can insert a *codicil*, a supplementary document with clauses that either add to or revoke those in the original will. Under no circumstances should you make a change directly on the page of a will itself; this will invalidate the entire document or call into question your state of mind during the writing

You'll also need to check with your state to see if there are any additional requirements for the process of validating your will and to make sure that there are no specific restrictions on the transfer of property from estate to beneficiary. For instance, while in most states divorce automatically revokes a will with regard to the ex-spouse, in New Hampshire and a few other states a divorced spouse is not automatically revoked. This means that an ex-spouse would lawfully be granted one-third to one-half of your estate, depending upon the laws of your state – including your animals. Most divorce decrees in these states do include a specific clause that revokes an ex-spouse's claim to property in the estate of the other spouse, but you do want to be doubly sure that this issue is addressed. If you live in one of these states and don't want your pets to go to an ex-spouse who always resented the attention you paid to the animals during your marriage, you'll need to include a provision in your will and divorce decree that specifically states that the animals shall not be given to that person.

EUTHANASIA?

You may find it difficult to believe, but there are actually pet owners out there who include in their wills a clause directing the executor to destroy their pets upon their death.

There are several motivations behind this kind of decision. One is that the owner feels that the pet would be so miserable without him that the only logical thing to do is to choose euthanasia. Another reason may be that the owner is not familiar with the idea of planning for PerPETual Care, has no friends or family to take his pets, and knows the risk is high that the animal would end up in a shelter for a few terrifying days before being euthanized anyway due to its unadoptability. Yet another is the owner's belief that no adoptive home or living situation could ever match the quality of the pets' current home. In order to prevent the pet from living in a less-than-stellar household, he decides to forestall all that and euthanize the pet.

Fortunately, if someone – the executor, a family member, or friend – objects to putting the animal down, past cases show that the probate court judge tends to side with the dissenter. In addition, probate courts tend to rule against wills that direct the executor to destroy any of the deceased's property, whether the property refers to pets or television sets.

However, it's important to realize that in the process of naming a permanent caretaker for your pet, you are essentially passing along a piece of property. It is the pets' new owner who *does* possess the right to do with the animal as he pleases, which could feasibly include euthanasia. Although most pet lovers would find this to be highly unlikely, it's another argument for using great discretion in choosing your caretaker.

THE LAST WORD

Regardless of the details you include in your will about the future care of your pets, it's important to keep in mind that there are certain legal requirements you'll need to fulfill in drawing up your will so that it is recognized as valid by the court. This means that it has to be typed, witnessed, signed, and notarized. You'll also need to make sure that it satisfies any particular regulations that are law in your own state. In some states, holographic – or handwritten and generally unwitnessed – wills are valid, while in others they will be dismissed out of hand. Likewise, once upon a time oral wills were recognized as valid "documents."

As is the case with choosing a primary caretaker and an alternate guardian, you'll need to make sure that your intentions and the wording in your will are crystal clear, not just regarding your pets but every part of your estate. There have been numerous legal challenges when a pet owner has specified that a certain sum of money should be left to a pet caretaker in the event of the owner's death. However, if the will doesn't specifically state that this money is awarded only if the pet is still alive, the court will usually rule that the money should still be given to the appointed caretaker even if there's no pet to spend it on. As is so frequently the case in legal concerns, the addition or subtraction of a word or two can mean all the difference in the eyes of the law. Be careful and have a lawyer review the final document for accuracy and intent.

What To Do Now

- Understand why you'll need more than a will as part of your PerPETual Care plan.
- If you do draw up a will, arrange for an interim guardian to care for your pets for the period between your death and the validation of your will by the court.
- In selecting the executor of your will, be sure that she will always consider the welfare of your pets to be of utmost importance.
- Review the PerPETual Care clauses and conditions in your will at least once a year to account for changes in the lives of your executor and caretakers.
- Make sure that your will leaves no doubt as to your intent and is prepared in accordance with the laws of your state.

6

In Dog — Or Cat — We Trust

Just as the writer of a will cannot name a pet as a direct beneficiary, a pet owner who draws up a trust is also forbidden to leave property directly to her furry loved ones. You'll recall that the law regards pets as property, and property cannot own property. So as is the case with supporting your pets through a will, you'll still have to involve humans to carry out your wishes: one to act as trustee to administer the funds and another person to serve as your pets' primary caretaker.

Unlike a will, however, when it comes to providing Per-PETual Care for a pet via a trust, the courts have regarded these arrangements a bit more favorably in many cases. Indeed, many state legislatures have recently passed laws that allow people to specifically set up a trust to provide funds that will allow a caretaker to look after a surviving pet. In fact, trusts have a long history of serving as a suitable vehicle for caring for a pet after death. One of the earliest cases to involve a court challenge to a person's estate involving a trust bequest for the care of a pet occurred in Kentucky in 1923, where the state Supreme Court ruled in favor of the animal.

However, many courts have invalidated trusts for the care of pets because they violated a legal tenet known as the *rule against perpetuities*. Essentially, the law states that in order to be valid, a trust needs to have a limited lifespan that is measured in human years – usually 21 years – after which it ceases to exist. Since pet trusts measure the lives of their beneficiaries in – no surprise here – pet years, many an aggrieved relative, resentful that their aunt was more generous with a dog or cat than with a human, has managed to get a pet trust invalidated.

One way around the issue of pet trusts in the past was for the court to consider a pet trust to be an *honorary trust,* where the judge leaves it up to the honor of the trustee to enforce the trust.

Today, the revision of the Uniform Probate Code – outlined in Appendix C – and new laws regulating pet trusts in many states have either changed the rule against perpetuities by extending the period of 21 years, specifically stating that the trust lasts until the pet dies, or have eliminated any mention of length of years.

Trusts 101

Essentially, a trust is a type of account that can hold both property and money. The person who creates the trust can be variously known as a *settler, trustor,* or *grantor,* and assigns a *trustee* to administer the trust and to disburse the funds and/or property to a *beneficiary,* who receives the proceeds from the trust. The property is legally referred to as the *principal,* or *corpus.*

Every trust falls into one of two categories before splitting off to become more specialized: You can stipulate in your will that you wish to create a *testamentary trust* that only takes effect at your death, or you can opt for a *living trust,* also known as an *inter vivos trust,* which you establish and activate while you're still alive. A living trust is sometimes referred to as a "will substitute." A variation on a living trust is a revocable living trust, which allows the grantor to amend the trust at any time, adding or removing property, or even revoking the trust completely. If the living trust is not specifically a revocable living trust, the grantor is powerless to change it at any point. Of course, since a testamentary trust is created upon the grantor's death, changing it is not an option and therefore it is always irrevocable.

With a living trust, you can add property at any time during your lifetime and also stipulate in your will that certain property from your estate will be added to it upon your death. The major advantage of a living trust is that it does not have to go through probate court; in other words, the people and pets you deem to be your heirs can receive the property in your trust immediately upon your death, instead of waiting several months or longer to receive it, which could obviously be a life-or-death matter when it comes to your pets. Another benefit to a living trust is that it's totally private. Heirs and the public-at-large will not know how your assets are distributed or what they consist of; all cases that go through probate court are a matter of public record. A testamentary trust is also subject to probate.

Another way a living trust can be a big plus is that it can

be written in such a way that if you become disabled for an extended period of time, you can draw on funds from the trust that will pay a guardian to take care of your pet until you're able to step in again.

The major drawback to either a living or testamentary trust is that it tends to be more expensive to draft than a simple will, due to its complexity. A will can be as brief as a couple of pages while the average trust consists of 25 to 30 pages. However, in the end, the savings from avoiding probate more than pays for a trust, since paying the legal fees required to proceed through probate can easily consume 5 percent of an estate's value, sometimes more.

Because of the complexity of trusts and the need to comply with particular state laws, I wouldn't recommend that you tackle the writing of a trust yourself. Educate yourself about trusts as much as possible, however, so that you're well prepared to discuss all your options with an attorney who specializes in trusts. One good book is *The Truth About Trusts,* by Jack W. Everett, published by FTPC Publishing.

DIFFERENT KINDS OF TRUSTS
Here's the lowdown on several other kinds of trusts:

Charitable Remainder Trust
Upon the creation of this trust, all the property you transfer into it will be donated to a charity that you specify. This charity must have tax-exempt status with the I.R.S. and typically requires an initial funding of $100,000 or more in order to make the tax and income advantages worth it.

Honorary Trust
Courts sympathetic to the plight of animals orphaned by an owner's death have tended to view a trust drawn up to sup-

port a pet as an honorary trust, where the named trustee is not compelled to administer the trust. In addition, the trust is neither invalidated nor enforced by the court. In other words, the tenets laid out in an honorary trust obviously rely on the goodwill of the trustee to carry out the grantor's wishes. With an honorary trust, if the trustee decides not to administer the funds for the pet, the money earmarked for the care goes back into the trust to be distributed as part of the residual property; that is, the property that is not specifically listed in the trust.

Pooled Charitable Income Trust

This is a trust set up by a charity that then solicits donations from people who don't have the funds to set up a traditional charitable remainder trust. Initial donations can be as low as $5,000, with subsequent donations in $1,000 increments. The advantage of a pooled charitable income trust is that the charity pays donors income on a regular basis and donors receive a tax deduction for part of each donation that is made to the fund. This brand of trust resembles a mutual fund: the charity has more money and ways to invest, and donors are able to reap the benefits of that larger pooled investment. Upon your death, the charity then receives the full amount of your donation outright, and, as a condition of donating regularly to the fund, you can negotiate with the charity to have them draw on part of it in order to support your pets in the manner that you specify.

HOW STATES DIFFER

Although the laws about probate are different in each state, there are general guidelines that all 50 states follow. A legal entity known as the Uniform Probate Code essentially dictates how probate is regarded and how estates are processed throughout the country. State legislatures are generally free to adopt the code, table it for further study, or ignore it. In 1990, the National Conference of Commissioners on Uniform State Laws added a section to the Uniform Probate Code that would validate "a trust for the care of a designated domestic or pet animal and the animal's offspring."

The full text of the Code can be found in Appendix C; a list of states that have legalized pet trusts, along with the exact statutes, appears in Appendix D.

If your state hasn't passed a pet trust law based on the Uniform Probate Code, an honorary trust would probably work for you, or you can use any one of the other planning tools described in PerPETual Care. You may also want to do some legal research to locate challenges to pet trusts in your state in recent years. Check to see how the court ruled to determine how your trust would hold up in the future. Hopefully, by the time it's needed, pet trusts will be a federal law, but you need to be doubly sure when drawing up a PerPETual Care plan for your pets.

CHOOSING A TRUSTEE

Just as you need to take utmost care in selecting an executor for your will who will have your pets' best interest in mind, so too you need to carefully select the person who will be in charge of administering your trust, known as the trustee. The trustee will write the checks for your pets' upkeep – either directly to the veterinarian and groomer and pet store – or pay a lump sum to the caretaker, who will then be responsible for paying all bills with the money entrusted to her. The trustee will also be responsible for making sure that the caretaker you've chosen has your pets' best interests at heart and is following your instructions as close to the letter as possible. In your trust, you should specifically give the trustee the power to select another caretaker if the trustee feels that your first choice is not living up to her end of the deal, or if the caretaker declares she is not able to care for your pets.

It goes without saying that your trustee should be an animal lover. Frequently, people appoint either their personal attorney or an officer at the bank to serve as trustee, without knowing whether they even have a pet of their own.

You'll also need to select an alternate trustee in case your first choice is unable to serve.

LIMITATIONS OF A PET TRUST

As you've already learned, the rule against perpetuities has forced people to get creative about designing a pet trust that works, but another, more serious, disadvantage of a pet trust involves animals that are renowned for their longevity, like parrots and horses. Many states place a limit of 21 years on a trust's lifetime; after that, the trust must be dissolved, with any remaining funds going to the beneficiary or other party named by the creator of the trust. If the animal is still alive, tough luck.

If, however, you live in a state that recognizes pet trusts and has stated that the trust shall be in effect until the end of the pet's natural life, then a lengthy lifespan does not present a problem. If you live in a pet-trust-unfriendly state, however, you'll need to consider other ways to fund your pets' care, including a lump sum payout from a life insurance policy to a sanctuary that specializes in long-lived animals. In fact, it's a good idea to ask the directors of these sanctuaries for their advice. No doubt they've dealt with these issues before and will have ideas about the best way to solve your dilemma. In any case, you may have to forget about using a trust to fund your plans if you live in a state where the trust would be invalidated after twenty-one years.

How Much Do You Need?

Again, as is the case with the money you leave in your will to a beneficiary for your pets, it's important not to leave anything to chance. Be sure to fund the trust with enough money to take care of all reasonable expenses and incidentals throughout the expected lifespan of your pet, but do not overfund it to such an extent that other beneficiaries will feel they've been shortchanged in favor of your pets. While wills are challenged far more than trusts, you still run the risk of having a judge overrule your wishes if you fund a trust with an excessive amount of money, keeping in mind the funds necessary to maintain the standard of living your pets enjoyed while you were alive. Again, use your best judgment and the advice of an attorney to come up with a figure that will stand up in court if the trust is challenged.

What will become of the money that's left over when your pet dies? If a nonprofit animal organization is serving as your primary caretaker, it's best to name that same group as your remainder beneficiary, as the individual or group who receives the remaining money is known. If the trust provides income to the group as administered by your trustee, upon the deaths of all of your pets covered under the trust the organization will receive the remaining funds and the trust will be dissolved. If you have a friend or family member who will serve as your pets' caretaker, however, it's still a good idea to name a nonprofit group as the remainder beneficiary. Though it's not pleasant to consider the possibility, a caretaker who regards the trust money as one big jackpot may feel compelled to end a pet's life in order to collect the payout sooner. Of course, it's unlikely, but you want to be sure your pets are taken care of to the end of their natural lives.

What To Do Now

- Learn about the different kinds of trusts that exist for estate planning of all kinds.
- Decide whether a trust would work best for your Per-PETual Care plans.
- Check to see whether your state recognizes legalized pet trusts or whether the courts have a record of recognizing the need for trusts for PerPETual Care.
- Talk with an attorney with experience writing trusts; don't write it yourself.
- When selecting a trustee to administer your pet trust, make sure the person will be steadfast about carrying out your wishes.
- If you have a pet like a parrot or horse, think twice about choosing a trust for their PerPETual Care plans, due to the longevity of these animals.
- To avoid a possible challenge by a relative, don't over-fund your pet trust.

7

Gimme Shelter:
Sanctuaries and
Retirement Homes

The idea of a retirement home for pets probably strikes non-pet lovers in the same way that most special items for dogs, cats, parrots, horses, iguanas, ferrets, fish, and other household pets hits them: extravagant and just a bit ridiculous.

Admittedly, there may be more than a few pet lovers who will tend to agree with the pet agnostics on this point, maybe even you. But if you stop and think about it, a special place where well-loved pets can live out the remainder of their years in the company of similar animals as well as with humans who love them makes a tremendous amount of sense, especially if their owner has died. Plus, as you'll discover, anyone who signs up their furry loved ones for a pet retirement home will be supporting a good cause.

Although pet retirement homes and sanctuaries have not yet caught on in the public consciousness, there are enough of them that they do indeed come in many different forms and are run by a variety of organizations, both nonprofit and privately-run. The best part of these homes is that, in most cases, the animals can roam free throughout the house or their designated living area; they're not confined to living in a cage for the rest of their lives.

How They're Different

Just like retirement homes for their human counterparts, pet retirement facilities and sanctuaries come in many different stripes. Many are rural, where space to build dog runs and horse pastures is not at a premium, though there are also many pet retirement homes in suburban areas and even in cities. Some emphasize finding a new home for pets in their care while others promise the owner that this will be the last home for the pet.

If you find the idea of a retirement home for your pets' PerPETual Care residence appealing, you'll inevitably discover even more differences between them once you start doing a little bit of research. For now, here's the general lowdown on what's currently out there.

Shelter-Run Home

In recent years, some of the larger humane societies in populated metropolitan areas have developed or set aside separate buildings that serve as long-term cat condos or dog kennels for pets whose owners have died or entered a nursing home. These owners tend to be long-standing members of the shelter or humane organization, or have designated a donation to the shelter from their estate after they die in exchange for agreeing to care for their pets until the animals die.

Of course, this idea is not new, as pet owners have long held individual agreements with animal nonprofits. The concept first began to take hold when shelters realized that this kind of donation agreement could provide them with a steady source of funds – through an annuity or flat payment – that could, if multiplied, pay for a large chunk of their operating budgets. In the past, the pets may have lived in the staff area or had the general run of the shelter, and they may or may not have been earmarked for adoption if the right person came along. Today, more shelters have gotten organized and are developing programs that cater to this group by setting aside property just for these trust-fund pets.

Some of these groups include the Associated Humane Society in New Jersey, which include Kitty City and Animal Haven Farm, and Bide-A-Wee's Golden Years Retirement Home in Westhampton, New York. More are listed in Appendix A, complete with contact information.

Veterinarian-Affiliated Home

Whoever first came up with the idea of running a pet retirement home in connection with a veterinary school should get a medal of some kind. Several problems are solved at once: Pets get a permanent homelike environment to live out their years along with very close medical attention, the veterinary school receives income via an endowment, students receive scholarship money and/or a place to live, and the veterinary program has a supply of animals to study and work with on a long-term basis. The benefits depend upon the program and venue, but the important thing is that everyone wins.

The "home" may be a private single-family home near the campus or a separate wing in an institutional-style school building. One veterinary school is even starting to request that future donors consider bequeathing their homes to the school, as a way to build a network of pet retirement homes throughout the state. Any pets, of course, would be allowed to live out their years in the home they're accustomed to, though they may need to share it with a few more animal companions through the years.

Two schools with pet retirement homes include Texas A&M University and the University of Minnesota College of Veterinary Medicine. Contacts for these and others are in Appendix A.

Breed- or Pet-Specific Sanctuary
Although there are boarding kennels that accept both dogs and cats, many people who own just cats have discovered the hard way that if their feline kids have to be boarded for a short time, they much prefer an environment without dogs. Some dogs, of course, could care less while others would love to have cat companions. However, many cat lovers appreciate the skill and attitude that come from a kennel keeper who "knows" cats. Indeed, on the few occasions I've had to board cats at mixed dog-and-cat facilities, the cats were largely ignored and, when they returned home, the residual trauma took a few days to shake off.

This same philosophy holds true as the impetus behind a pet owner's decision to choose a retirement home or sanctuary that accepts only their type of pet. A certain environment is expected – and much appreciated – by some owners who know how uncomfortable their pets can be around other unfamiliar types of animals. In these specialized homes you can expect that the owner and staff are truly cat people, or bird people, which goes a long way in helping any new arrival feel at home as quickly as possible.

Environment obviously plays a huge role in the develop-

ment and existence of special sanctuaries for horses and
birds. In fact, retreats for these animals have been around a
lot longer than the up-and-coming brand of dog and cat retirement homes. The primary reason is that it tends to be the
rule that a tropical bird or horse will outlive its owner –
some of these retirement homes have actually been around
for decades.

A few examples of breed- and pet-specific sanctuaries in-
clude Aledos Riverside Ranch for horses, in Random Lake,
Wisconsin, and the Wild Cat Ranch in Comfort, Texas.
Many more can be found in Appendix A.

Privately Run Home: Nonprofit

If you've ever volunteered at your local humane society or
have otherwise been involved in helping homeless animals,
whether transporting them from a kill shelter to their new
home or donating money to a national organization, then
you're aware of how that one small foot in the door can
quickly get to the point where you're turning a couple of
rooms in your home into wards for fostering abandoned pup-
pies and kittens to serving on the board of the local shelter.
Working with animals in need can quickly expand to consume all of your free time, or even cause you to switch ca-
reers into the humane field.

This situation is frequently responsible for how people
end up as chief cook and bottlewasher running a nonprofit
pet retirement facility in their own home. In one instance,
one woman started a nonprofit rescue organization out of her
home in order to deduct the thousands of dollars she was
already shelling out for vet bills and food each year. As her
reputation spread, of course, she found lots of unwanted animals dumped on her doorstep each year, but she also helped
owners reunite with pets they thought were lost forever.

When a grateful owner left her $10,000 in his will with the stipulation that she take in his cat Pookie for the rest of the pet's natural life, a retirement home was tacked onto the seemingly endless list of humane services she already provided to the community, and a new niche was born.

Sometimes these homes are run by one person, while others are operated in conjunction with fully-staffed rescue organizations. Two such homes include Last Chance for Life in Oklahoma City and The Home for Life Animal Sanctuary in Star Prairie, Wisconsin. More in Appendix A.

Privately Run Home: For-Profit
This last category is probably the most common type of retirement home, but also the least-known. Often instituted as an extension of a professionally run dog or cat kennel or pet-sitting business as an extra service to favored and long-time customers, a retirement home run in this fashion is also the most informal. A separate building is probably not an option for pets in need of a home after an owner dies or is unable to care for his animals any longer. Instead, the "retired" pets are most likely integrated into the household and treated like one of the gang. This is an ideal option for pets accustomed to living with other pets and having lots people around, but not for animals that have previously lived as the only pet in a household. The chances of the animal being adopted out are slim in most of these situations.

Because it is so informal, you'll need to approach the pet professionals who know you and your pets to see if they would agree to take in your pets if something happens to you. It may be an entirely new concept for them, so lend them a copy of this book when you're done with it, or have them buy wholesale copies to give to their favorite customers. Both of you will need to agree on an adequate stipend in exchange for taking in your pets under a PerPETual Care arrangement.

COMPARE AND CONTRAST

If you were placing your own mother or father into a nursing home or senior care center, of course you would shop around, visit each one personally, and try to get detailed references from professionals and other people in your situation. You should do no less when choosing a sanctuary or retirement home for your pets.

Perhaps the most important issue to consider is whether the place will still be around in a few years, or indeed, a few decades. Those pet retirement homes and sanctuaries run in conjunction with humane organizations that have a good reputation, are well-staffed, and have significant funding are the most likely to survive through both tight times and flush. The downside is that in order to accomplish this they may accept more animals into their retirement program than is suitable for the facility in terms of space and number of staffers and/or volunteers. However, many homes and sanctuaries do have a self-directed limit on how many animals can live in a particular facility or to maintain a certain ratio of pets to each staff member.

Despite the apparent stability of some of the larger homes you may be researching, you shouldn't automatically rule out the smaller pet retirement homes that may have only been around for a few years. This does a disservice to the dedication and love of animals of many of the people who run these one-person operations. Research the background of the home's founder and, if you visit the facility – which is strongly recommended – spend at least the day there to see how the owner and staff interact with the resident animals.

You will undoubtedly want to fully research any home

you're considering. Here's a list of questions you'll want to ask before you agree to have a home or sanctuary accept your pets:

- How long have they been in business, with both the retirement home and any ancillary animal-related businesses? How many pets have come to live there over the last year?
- What fee do you expect to receive for my pets, given their current ages?
- What kind of food do you provide for the residents, and how often do you feed them?
- What if my pets are on a special kind of diet? Will that cost extra?
- Which veterinary clinic do you work with? How far away is their office? What criteria do you use to determine whether a resident needs to see the vet? (Here, it's a good idea to ask to see the veterinary records of a pet that's lived in the home for at least a couple of years, in order to see what types of situations causes a vet visit; however, in addition to records from the primary veterinarian who works with the home, the facility itself should also keep a file on each pet that records this information.)
- How often are the pets supervised during the day and night so that medical emergencies can be acted on without delay?
- How much human attention do the pets receive on a daily basis?
- How are pets of different ages, temperaments, and breeds exercised each day?
- Where do the residents spend the majority of their

day? Are they allowed to roam freely throughout one part of the home or are they confined to cages when staff are absent?

- Are all outdoor play areas fully fenced and secured to protect against predators and escape?
- Does the home keep pets until their deaths, or do they attempt to adopt out some of the pets to new owners? If my pet is adopted, what will happen to the remaining fee I've paid to you? What if I don't want anyone to adopt my pets?
- What plans do you have to place the animals should you need to close down the business?
- What do you do when my pets die? (Correct answer: Whatever you tell them to do, as you'll discover in the next chapter when you'll make your plans for your pets' final resting place.)

And so on. You'll be able to come up with more questions on your own concerning your pets' own needs and personalities.

WHY DO THEY COST SO MUCH?

Once you start to investigate different PerPETual Care programs at retirement homes and sanctuaries, you'll probably marvel at the wide range of fees and donations that facilities charge to accept pets into their programs. I've seen the cost vary from $5,000 to $25,000 per pet. Why do they charge so much when the annual budget for just Squatter, an elderly special needs cat at that, comes to just over $500? Besides, those programs deal in volume, which means they get their supplies and services in bulk at cheaper rates.

In some wills and trusts where one person bequeaths one pet to another, I've seen the sum of money given to support that pet range from $1,000 to $5,000 per year; in other cases, that same one to five thousand dollars could serve as a lump sum to cover one pet's lifetime. Why the great difference between an individual caretaker and a facility?

For one, the sanctuaries and retirement homes have business expenses that include staff salaries, the overhead of a building plus utilities, food, veterinary bills, insurance, marketing costs to get the word out, and other costs of doing business. The cost per pet could easily run to several thousand dollars a year or more.

On the other hand, I've seen a few retirement homes and sanctuaries that set their fees according to the age of a pet upon admission. Obviously, longevity is something you'll need to consider; many facilities tend to use the age of 18 as a benchmark for many pets, and figure on a particular budget for each pet per year, increasing the fee appropriate per year as the pet ages.

You may be surprised at the fees, but then again, many retirement homes and sanctuaries use the money not only to support your pets but also to keep their own programs going strong, taking in unwanted and abandoned animals and supporting community programs, and footing the bill themselves.

Anyway, you can't take it with you, so you might as well leave it for the animals.

WHAT TO DO NOW

- Learn about the different kinds of retirement homes and sanctuaries available for your pets' PerPETual Care plans.
- Think about which home or sanctuary would make for the best fit for your pets.

- Consider the differences between the retirement homes and sanctuaries that appeal to you most.
- Ask lots of specific questions when interviewing the owner of a prospective pet retirement home or sanctuary. And be sure to take a copy of the list in this chapter with you.

8

The Fine Print: What Else You Can Do

So now what? You've learned about the many different ways you can make sure your pets are well taken care of if you're not there to do it, and you probably have a good sense of what would work best for everyone involved: you, your proposed caretaker, and your pet.

And yet, something's still nagging at you. You're not 100 percent sure of your choice, and really, do you have to do it now? After all, you've put it off for years already, what harm can another couple of weeks – or months – do?

Plenty. Can you answer with perfect certainty that if you were to step in front of a bus tomorrow that you know your pets would go to good homes and be able to live out their natural lives? I'd have to guess that you do have your doubts – after all, you did pick up this book in the first place. Come on, you've gotten this far, you're almost there. For the sake of your pets, you have to finish up. All that's left for you to do is to finalize your decision.

Too Many Choices?

Maybe your problem is that all the choices you've read about sound good. Your niece has agreed to take care of your pets. She loves animals and has volunteered at her local animal shelter since high school. However, the director at your local humane society has gotten so inspired since your conversation with him about securing the future of your pets that he's now planning a PerPETual Care program of his own, and it would be great to be the first to sign up. Yet, a retirement home for your pets sounds good, too.

How will you decide?

When it comes to choosing the best PerPETual Care plan for each of your pets, sometimes it all comes down to how to leave your biggest mark on the world, at least when it involves animals. If something were to happen to you tomorrow and you had appointed your niece to serve as caretaker, which then spurred her on to attend veterinary school and save many hundreds of animals' lives over the years, then your mark would be large indeed.

On the other hand, maybe you're aware that your local humane society has been working on a plan to convert to a no-kill shelter, but they need funds in order to implement it. If you work with them on a plan where you'd donate all the money from a $250,000 life insurance policy in exchange for providing PerPETual Care for your pets, then that mark would be extremely significant in your own community. Of course, after solidifying your plans, if you and your pets live a long and happy life, chances are they would receive those funds decades after they've already instituted a no-kill shelter. In that case, you could then work with them on a Plan B to accomplish other seemingly impossible tasks with the funds you plan to leave them.

Then again, it may all come down to the money. In purely financial tones, do you want or need a tax break now and are you able to make the PerPETual Care donations before you die, or will the funds come out of your estate? Tax constraints, of course, are an important issue when making a donation to a charity. If you want to place your pets in a nonprofit sanctuary or retirement home, the matter of whether you can prepay the tax-deductible fee before death – either in full or in stages – or whether they only accept it after your demise may play into the decision you make. Indeed, if you have few assets during your lifetime and plan for a life insurance policy to fund your PerPETual Care plans, then it seems your primary decision is to choose a caretaker.

Still can't decide? Then it's time to let your pets make the decision for you.

WHY YOUR PETS NEED A LAST WILL & TESTAMENT

Don't laugh. Though you have your own ideas about the best caretaker and living situation for your pets, it's obviously important to listen to how your pets weigh in on the matter. If you let your pets develop their own PerPETual Care plans, what would they say? You know your pets better than anyone, and once you start to write a last will and testament for each animal by getting inside their heads, as it were, you may be surprised at what they say when they're given the chance.

Strictly speaking, it's not exactly a will, but more like a document where your pet can voice her desires about where she would like to live and who she'd prefer to serve as her replacement human can opener if something should happen to you.

Needless to say, have some fun with this one. You don't need to write in a formal style – just pretend you're one of your pets and you're sitting down to write your will, complete with all the quirks and personality of that particular pet. Here's the will I wrote for Rula Lenska, a seven-year-old female Maine Coon cat.

I, Rula Lenska, being of catnipped mind and feline body, do hereby leave my nail clippers to Squatter, who will never need them, my favorite soggy catnip mouse to Bunny, who will stink it up even more with her breath than I ever did, and my grooming brush to Mush, who always liked it more than I did.

I leave the computer desk light turned on for Black Kitty, because I always managed to elbow her out of the way when she was basking under it. To Sweetie, I leave my twice-daily portion of wet stinky cat food, because that boy needs some meat on his bones. To Nicky, my comrade Maine Coon, I leave him the mantle of being the sole longhaired cat in the household.

To Pippy, my buddy since kittenhood, I leave the bathroom faucet leaking forever, since that's where you spend half of your waking hours.

However, if my primary human can opener should run out of her one life before I run out of my nine, here's what I would like:

I don't mind the six new additions you've moved in here in the last year, and it would be okay if you were to keep us all together. After all, I get some good exercise every day from chasing Demon Kitty and Black Kitty just to remind them that I was here before they arrived on the scene. If you have to split us up, I would like to keep the original Gang of Six together (Me, Pippy, Mush, Bunny, Squatter, and yes, even Beast). Since we've been hanging out so long, there are no surprises, and we all know our place in the pecking order and don't try to mess around with it too much.

Where would I like us all to live? I like Gregg, and rumor has it that his house is twice as big as ours with lots of room for daily Kitty Olympics events, but I'm not crazy about that cat smell you bring back with you after you've deserted us for a night to go play with those high-strung snob cats at Gregg's Abyssinian Asylum. Where do they get off, anyway, acting so high and mighty when they've all been abandoned at least a couple of times? But I could give it a shot since all those boys clearly need some female authority over there.

If Gregg's house doesn't work out, I don't want to live in a cage, so I don't want to live in a shelter while I wait to approve of my new home. The time I had to have emergency surgery, I was in pain, not only from the stitches but from the indignity of being confined to a cage. If I have to live in one room while I wait, I can deal with that, so a temporary foster home would work for a month or so.

Just don't send me to your sister's in New Jersey, I know dog when I smell it, and that's not only dog smell, it's puppy smell, so you might as well forget that arrangement.

A retirement home sounds good too, as long as I have free reign over the house. You know how bored I get from being in one spot: First I sleep in the morning sun in the living

83

room, then nap in the foyer in the cat tree at noon, then doze in the window napper in the downstairs bathroom until dinnertime. And remember, southern exposure is vital for any home you choose – you know how much I like my sun.

I guess that's all for now. Just remember to keep that catnip coming!

And so on. As is the case with the other PerPETual Care plans, try to write a will for each of your pets. It may prove to be a big help in helping you make your decision.

Living Wills for Pets

What are your thoughts about needlessly keeping your pets alive when sick or injured? If you've had to watch while a beloved pet became too ill to enjoy his life and he needed your assistance to eat, drink, and even walk with his usual dignity, you knew that it was time to peacefully end his life, however difficult the task seemed.

When you finalize a PerPETual Care plan for each of your pets, it's your duty to pass on your personal ideas about euthanasia to the new caretaker of your pets. It can be something simple, a short paragraph on a separate piece of paper tucked into each PerPETual Care kit you prepare. If you have any firm ideas about whether you want your pets cremated or buried, this is the place to include this information as well.

If Eclipse should become sick and need help to eat and drink and has noticeable difficulty in going up and down the stairs and using the litter box; in other words, if his normal daily routines become painful for him, I request that his caretaker choose euthanasia to relieve his misery.

You should also tuck a copy of this document in with the PerPETual Care kits you provide to your veterinarian to complete her records for each pet.

VETERINARY HEALTH INSURANCE

While we're on the topic of the health of your pets, if you're relying on a friend or family member to serve as your PerPETual Care guardian for your pets, you'll want to make things as easy as possible. Purchasing a veterinary health insurance policy for each of your pets is a good idea, especially if you're providing little or no money to fund the care and even more so if your pets are older.

If you choose a retirement home or veterinary school-based home, the organization inevitably includes health care and medication in as part of the fee you pay, so this won't be a concern. However, even if you're planning to live a long life along with your pets, you just might consider signing up for veterinary health insurance for your pets today.

PERPETUAL CARE FOR EVERYONE

Well, the hard work is over. You now know what you need to do to make sure that nothing will happen to any of your beloved pets in the event that something should happen to you.

Make sure you draw up complete PerPETual Care kits for all of your animals. Create new ones when additional pets come to live with you and update the kits you have for all of your pets whenever necessary. And be sure to enjoy your pets while you're both still around.

Now get busy! After all, your pets can't wait.

What To Do Now

- If you can't decide on the best PerPETual Care plan, consider which would have the most impact for all animals.
- Have each pet write his own Last Will and Testament.
- Write out a living will for each pet.
- Consider purchasing veterinary health insurance.
- Enjoy your pets every day while you can.

Appendix A:
Sanctuaries and
Retirement Homes

J ust as there are different kinds of retirement homes for people, a wide variety exists for pets as well. Some accept everything that flies, crawls, or walks upright, while others restrict their homes to one kind of pet; some even take in just one breed.

The following homes are broken down into categories and arranged alphabetically by state. Keep in mind that this is just a directory, a reference tool for your convenience. By including these homes on the list, you should not imply that I recommend one over another, and if one is missing from the list, it simply means I didn't know about it.

In fact, if you notice that I've left one off the list that you're familiar with, you can send an email with pertinent contact information and all the details to me via email at updates@PerPETualcarebook.com, and I'll try to add it to the next edition of *PerPETual Care*.

General Pet Retirement Homes & Programs
California
Animal Helpline
Judith Lindley
P.O. Box 944
Morongo Valley CA 92256
619-363-6511

Guardians for Life
Marin Humane Society
171 Bel Marin Keys Boulevard
Novato CA 94949
415-883-4621
www.MarinHumaneSociety.org

Sido Service
San Francisco SPCA
2500 16th Street
San Francisco CA 94103
415-554-3000
www.sfspca.org

Colorado
Companion Care for Life Program
Humane Society of Boulder Valley
2323 55th Street
Boulder CO 80301
303-442-4030
www.boulderhumane.org

Iowa
The Noah's Ark Animal Foundation
P.O. Box 748

Fairfield IA 52556
515-472-0701
www.noahsark.org

NEW YORK
Bide-A-Wee Home Association
Golden Years Retirement Home
410 East 38th Street
New York NY 10016
212-532-6395
www.bideawee.org

North Shore Animal League
25 Davis Avenue
Port Washington NY 11050
516-883-7575
www.NSAL.org

WISCONSIN
Home For Life
Angel Care Program
Star Prairie WI
800-252-5918
www.homeforlife.org

BIRD RETIREMENT HOMES
COLORADO
The Gabriel Foundation
P.O. Box 11477
Aspen CO 81612
970-963-2620
www.thegabrielfoundation.org

GEORGIA
Feathered Friends Forever
2547 Misty Road
Appling GA 30802
706-541-9316

MASSACHUSETTS
Foster Parrots Ltd.
P.O. Box 650
Rockland MA 02370
781-878-3733
www.fosterparrots.com

MINNESOTA
Midwest Avian Adoption & Rescue Services
P.O. Box 821
Stillwater MN 55082
651-275-0568
www.maars.org

VIRGINIA
Rescue Me, An Avian Sanctuary
P.O. Box 534
Ark VA 23003
804-693-5997
www.rescueme.org

CAT RETIREMENT HOMES
ALASKA
Alaska Humane Society Adopt-A-Cat
P.O. Box 240587

Anchorage AK 99524
www.adopt-a-cat.org
907-344-8808

ARIZONA
The Hermitage No-Kill Cat Shelter
P.O. Box 13508
Tucson AZ 85732
520-571-7839
www.hermitagecats.org

CALIFORNIA
The Bluebell Foundation
20982 Laguna Canyon Road
Laguna Beach CA 92651
714-994-1586
www.bluebell.org

California Feline Foundation
500 North Van Ness
Fresno CA 93728
559-223-8690
www.valleyanimal.org

Friends of Cats Inc.
P.O. Box 1613
Lakeside CA 92040
www.friendsofcats.com

Living Free
54250 Keen Camp Road
Mountain Center CA 92561
909-659-4684

National Cat Protection Society
Retirement Centers
P.O. Box 6218
Long Beach CA 90806
714-650-1232
www.natcat.org

Pet Pride
P.O. Box 1055
Pacific Palisades CA 90272
www.petpride.org

Volunteers for Inter-Valley Animals
Sylvester House
P.O. Box 896
Lompoc CA 93438
805-735-6741
www.viva-animal-shelter.org

COLORADO
Cat Care Society
5985 West 11th Avenue
Lakewood CO 80214
303-239-9680
ww.catcaresociety.org

CONNECTICUT
The Last Post
P.O. Box 259
Falls Village CT 06031
860-824-0831

Appendix A

Hawaii
East Maui Animal Refuge
25 Maluaina Place
Haiku HI 96708
www.home.att.net/~ema_refuge

Illinois
Assisi Animal Foundation
P.O. Box 143
Crystal Lake IL 60039-0143
815-455-9411
www.assisi.org

Massachusetts
Bosler Humane Society
P.O. Box 520
Barre MA 01005
www.boslerhs.org

Michigan
Zimmer Foundation
TLC/for The Love of Cats
P.O. Box 130944
Ann Arbor MI 48113
734-663-8000
www.tlconline.org

Mississippi
Cedarhill Animal Sanctuary Inc.
144 Sanctuary Loop
Caledonia MS 39740
www.cedrhill.org

New Jersey
American Society for the Welfare of Cats
P.O. Box 594
Alloway NJ 08001
www.magpage.com/~jmagic/cats.html

Associated Humane Society
Kitty City
P.O. Box 43
Forked River NJ 08731
www.community.nj.com/HumaneSociety

New York
Kent Animal Shelter
2259 River Road
Calverton NY 11933
516-727-5731
www.kentanimalshelter.com

The Sunshine Home at This Old Cat
P.O. Box 320
Honeoye NY 14471
585-229-4790
www.thesunshinehome.com

Oklahoma
Last Chance for Life
P.O. Box 13190
Oklahoma City OK 73113

Rhode Island
The Hope for Animals Sanctuary of Rhode Island Inc.
P.O. Box 816

Slatersville RI 02876-0816
www.pet-net.net/hope_for_animals

TEXAS
Wild Cat Ranch
137 Upper Sisterdale Road
Comfort TX 78013
830-995-4689
www.wildcatranch.net

DOG RETIREMENT HOMES
ARKANSAS
Frank & Diana Stockton
194 Peta Lane
Mena AR 71953
501-394-1039

NEW YORK
Silver Streak Kennels
607-263-2007
www.dogretirement.com

OHIO
Circle Tail, Inc.
8834 Carey Lane
Pleasant Plain OH 45162
513-877-3325
www.circletail.org

Horse Retirement Homes
Alabama
S.A.G.E. Rescue Farm
Route 1 Box 234B
Dozier AL 36028

Arizona
Hooved Animal Humane Society of Arizona
P.O. Box 3025
Chino Valley AZ 86323
928-636-6026
www.hahsofaz.com

California
California Equine Retirement Fund
34033 Kooden Road
Winchester CA 92593
909-926-4190
www.crr-stable.com

IGHA/HorseAid
P.O. Box 6778 Eastview Station
Rancho Palos Verdes CA 90734-6778
310-719-9094
www.igha.org

Retire Your Horse
29598 East Shelton Rd
Linden CA 95236
209-887-9106
www.retireyourhorse.com

COLORADO
Colorado Horse Rescue
P O Box 1510
Arvada CO 80001
303-439-9217
www.chr.org

FLORIDA
Adopt-A-Horse, Ltd., Inc.
7609 West Josephine Road
Lake Placid FL 33852
www.adoptahorse.com

GEORGIA
Georgia Equine Rescue League, Ltd.
770-464-0138
www.gerlltd.org

ILLINOIS
Hooved Animal Humane Society
P.O. Box 400
Woodstock IL 60098
815-337-5563
www.hahs.org

MARYLAND
Horsenet Horse Rescue
2504 Arthur Ave
Eldersburg MD 21784
410-795-8989
www.horsenethorserescue.org

MICHIGAN
Hugs2Horses
P.O. Box 71
Fowlerville MI 48836
517-223-3263
www.hugs2horses.com

NEW HAMPSHIRE
Turtle Rock Rescue, Inc.
P.O. Box 156
Rindge NH 03461
603-899-6200
www.turtlerockrescue.com

NEW JERSEY
Mylestone Equine Rescue
227 Still Valley Road
Phillipsburg NJ 08865
908-995-9300
www.mylestone.org

NEW MEXICO
The Horse Shelter
100 AB Old Cash Ranch Road
Cerrillos NM 87010
505-984-3235

NEW YORK
The Second Chance Horse Rescue Inc.
6 Edgewood Drive
Central Valley NY 10917
845-928-6288
www.secondchancehorserescue.com

NORTH CAROLINA
The North Carolina Equine Rescue League
P.O. Box 352
Kernersville NC 27285
336-785-2430
www.ncerl.com

OHIO
Ohio Hooved Animal Humane Society
P.O. Box 1176
Hartville OH 44632
330-935-0117
www.ohahs.org

PENNSYLVANIA
Double D Equine Rescue
9312 Old Route 22
Bethel PA 19507
717-933-4648
www.ddrescue.org

SOUTH CAROLINA
SCARE, Inc.
Ridgeway SC 29130
888-866-8744
www.schorserescue.org

TEXAS
Habitat for Horses, Inc.
P.O. Box 213
Hitchcock TX 77563
409-935-0277
www.habitatforhorses.org

Second Chance Horse Refuge
11321 Morgan Drive
Nevada TX 75173
972-843-2100
www.secondchancehorserefuge.org

VIRGINIA
Dream Catcher Farm Horse Sanctuary
495 Adam Perry Road
Rocky Mount VA 24151
www.horsesanctuary.com

WASHINGTON
Second Chance Horse Rescue Ranch
25902 Hoehn Road
Sedro-Woolley WA 98284
360-856-4867
www.washingtonhorserescue.org

FARM ANIMAL RETIREMENT HOMES
CALIFORNIA
Amy's Farm
7698 Eucalyptus Ave
Chino CA 91710
909-393-2936
www.amysfarm.bigstep.com

MISSOURI
Humane Society of Missouri Farm
480 Josephs Road
Union MO 63084

636-583-8759
www.HSMO.org

VETERINARY PET RETIREMENT CENTERS
INDIANA
Purdue University School of Veterinary Medicine
School of Veterinary Medicine
Purdue University
1240 Lynn Hall
West Lafayette IN 47907-1240
765-494-0791
www.vet.purdue.edu

KANSAS
Office of Development
KSU College of Veterinary Medicine
103 Trotter Hall
1700 Denison Avenue
Manhattan KS 66506-5604
785-532-4833
www.vet.ksu.edu/depts/development/perppet.htm

MINNESOTA
University of Minnesota College of Veterinary Medicine
Kathleen McLaughlin
Director of Development
College of Veterinary Medicine
University of Minnesota
410 Veterinary Teaching Hospital
St. Paul MN 55108
612-624-6744
www.cvm.umn.edu

OKLAHOMA
Oklahoma State University
Development Office
308 McElroy Hall
Stillwater OK 74078-2011
405-744-5630
www.cvm.okstate.edu

TEXAS
Texas A&M University
Stevenson Companion Animal Life-Care Center
College Station TX 77843-4461
409-845-1188
www.cvm.tamu.edu

Appendix B:
Pet-Friendly
Legal Help

The following attorneys were located in the course of doing online research for *PerPETual Care*. They were found on various attorney referral websites such as www.lawyers.com and listed as having a specialty in animal law. Being included on this list does not serve as a recommendation, and I suggest that you interview at least two lawyers before paying a retainer.

ALABAMA
Gregory David Harrelson
The Southern Law Group, P.C.
3432 Old Columbiana Road
Birmingham AL 35226-3321
205-822-7800
www.southernlaw.org

Mark Sabel, Esquire
Sabel & Sabel, P.C.

2800 Zelda Road, Suite 100-5
Montgomery AL 36106
334-271-2770

ARIZONA
Maureen Beyers
Osborn Maledon, P.A.
2929 North Central Avenue, Suite 2100
Phoenix AZ 85012-2794
602-640-9000

Leslie F. Keehn
Robbins & Keehn
530 "B" Street, 24th Floor
San Diego CA 92101
619-232-1700

John G. Morrison
Morrison & Morrison
7130 East Stetson Drive
Scottsdale AZ 85251
480-990-9586

CALIFORNIA
David Blatte, Esquire
2161 Shattuck Avenue, Suite 227
Berkeley CA 94706
510-548-7382

Paige Gold, Esquire
2451 ½ West Silverlake Drive
Los Angeles CA 90039
213-507-6456

APPENDIX B

Sydney C. Kirkland
P.O. Box 1571
Los Gatos CA 95031
408-358-4529
www.sydneykirkland.com

Gregory J. Kohler
Kohler Law Office
1675 Chester Avenue, Suite 340
Bakersfield CA 93301
661-861-6045

Theresa J. Macellaro
Christensen, Miller, Fink, Jacobs, Glaser, Weil and Shapiro
2121 Avenue of the Stars, Eighteenth Floor
Los Angeles CA 90067
310-553-3000

Gary L. Moorhead
Pohlson, Moorhead & Goethals
23151 Moulton Parkway, Suite 102
Laguna Hills CA 92653
949-859-7070
www.orangecountyattorneys.net

Diane Parrish, Esquire
11684 Ventura Boulevard, Suite 320
Studio City CA 91607
818-766-5925

Robyn Ranke, Esquire
Blumberg, Lorber, Nelson LLP
137 North Acacia Avenue

Solana Beach CA 92075
858-509-0600
www.blnlaw.com

Andrew Ross, Esquire
251 South Lake Avenue, Suite 330
Pasadena CA 91101
626-568-2508

Michael Rotsten, Esquire
16133 Ventura Boulevard, Suite 900
Encino CA 91436
818-789-0256

Sarah Schmidt, Esquire
619 Woodworth Avenue, 2nd Floor
Clovis CA 93612

Robert J. Spitz
204 North San Antonio Avenue
Ontario CA 91762
909-395-0909

Bruce A. Wagman
One Market, Spear Street Tower, 32nd Floor
San Francisco CA 94105
415-901-8700

Sonia S. Waisman
Morrison & Foerster LLP
555 West Fifth Street, Suite 3500
Los Angeles CA 90013-1024
213-892-5200

APPENDIX B

CONNECTICUT
Nicole Bartner Graff
Suisman, Shapiro, Wool, Brennan, Gray & Greenberg, P.C.
2 Union Plaza, Suite 200
New London CT 06320
860-442-4416

FLORIDA
Jack L. Gordon, Esquire
Maney & Gordon, P.A.
101 East Kennedy Boulevard, Suite 3170
Tampa FL 33602
813-221-1366
www.maneygordon.com

Marcy I. LaHart, P.A.
711 Talladega Street
West Palm Beach FL 33405
561-655-9537

GEORGIA
Frank Brown, Esquire
Holland & Knight, LLP
1201 West Peachtree Street, N.E.
Atlanta GA 30309
404-898-8114

Gali Lynn Hagel
P.O. Box 680233
Marietta GA 30068-0004
770-578-3305

Sanford Wallack, Esquire
Michael Moran & Associates
852 R.D. Abernathy Boulevard, S.W.
Atlanta GA 30310
404-758-7500

ILLINOIS
Curtis L. Blood
1602 Vandalia
Collinsville IL 62234
618-345-4400

Amy A. Breyer
137 North Oak Park Avenue, Suite 400
Oak Park IL 60301
708-358-1400
www.AnimalLawOnline.net

Rick A. Halprin
542 South Dearborn Street, Suite 750
Chicago IL 60605-1525
312-697-0022

Neal H. Levin, Esquire
1970 North Halsted Street
Chicago IL 60614-5009
312-421-2100

KENTUCKY
Tomi Anne Blevins Pulliam
Seiller & Handmaker, LLP
462 South Fourth Avenue, Suite 2200
Louisville KY 40202

502-584-7400
www.derbycitylaw.com

LOUISIANA
Shawn Murray, Esquire
Chehardy, Sherman Law Firm
One Galleria Boulevard, Suite 1100
Metairie LA 70001
504-833-5600
www.ShawnMurray.com

Alan Prater, Esquire
Mills, Turansky & Cox
331 Milam Street, Suite 300
Shreveport LA 71166
318-222-0337
www.shreveportlegal.com

MARYLAND
Stephen L. Freedman
10019 Reisterstown Road, Suite 204
Owings Mills MD 21117
410-363-6848

Barbara R. Graham
103 North Adams Street
Rockville MD 20850
301-294-3467

MASSACHUSETTS
Richard D. Bickelman
Deutsch Williams Brooks DeRensis & Holland, P.C.
99 Summer Street

Boston MA 02110-1213
617-951-2300

Donna M. Turley
Macy & Turley, LLP
65A Atlantic Avenue
Boston MA 02110
617-720-4005

MICHIGAN
Acie G. Anderson, III
Bullard Anderson & Anderson, PLLC
6060 Dixie Highway, Suite H
Clarkston MI 48346-3476
248-623-3888

Stephen A. Seman, Esquire
1002 South Michigan Avenue
Saginaw MI 48602
989-790-0380

Linda Weiss, Esquire
Mount Pleasant MI 48858
989-772-3390

MINNESOTA
Ian Laurie, Esquire
Laurie & Laurie, P.A.
1660 South Highway 100
508 East Parkdale Plaza Building
Minneapolis MN 55416
952-738-0191

MISSOURI

Christopher Cox, Esquire
7751 Carondelet, Suite 401
St. Louis MO 63105
314-727-0163

Tonna Tharp Farrar
619 East 70th Street
Kansas City MO 64131
816-363-7100

MONTANA

Stefan T. Wall
Crowley, Haughey, Hanson, Toole & Dietrich
490 North 31st Street
Billings MT 59103
406-252-3441

NEBRASKA

Dan H. Ketcham
Engles, Ketcham, Olson & Keith, P.C.
1700 Farnam Street
Omaha NE 68102
402-348-0900

NEW HAMPSHIRE

Jennifer Eber, Esquire
Orr & Reno, P.A.
P.O. Box 3550
Concord NH 03302-3550

NEW JERSEY
Linda Sinuk, Esquire
71 Paterson Street
New Brunswick NJ 08901
732-296-1771

NEW YORK
John E. Bernacki, Jr.
11 State Street, Suite 200
Pittsford NY 14534
716-218-9550

Gary L. Francione
80 Business Park Drive, Suite 110
Armonk NY 10504
914-273-9800

Robert Friedlander, Esquire
299 Broadway, Suite 1405
New York NY 10007
212-227-1100

Marianne R. Merritt
Storch Amini & Munves, P.C.
405 Lexington Avenue, 51st Floor
New York NY 10174
212-490-4100

Rex M. Pietrobono
2 Sarles Street
Mount Kisco NY 10549
914-666-8137
www.nylawfirm.net

Patricia Rouse, Esquire
118-21 Queens Boulevard, Suite 306
Forest Hills NY 11375
718-268-0400
www.petlawandorder.com

Darryl M. Vernon
Vernon & Ginsburg, LLP,
261 Madison Avenue, 26th Floor
New York NY 10016-2303
212-949-7300

NORTH CAROLINA
Mary Margaret Nunalee
Nunalee & Nunalee, LLP
709 Princess Street
Wilmington NC 28402
910-254-1030
www.nunalaw.com

Kurt C. Stakeman
Womble Carlyle Sandridge & Rice
200 West Second Street
P.O. Drawer 84
Winston-Salem NC 27102
336-721-3600

OHIO
Gloria Rowland Homolak
6515 Olde York Road
Cleveland OH 44130
440-885-5599

Thomas William Lally
Belpar Law Center
4571 Stephen Circle, N.W.
Canton OH 44718-3629
330-499-5474

Richard M. Lewis
295 Pearl Street
P.O. Box 664
Jackson OH 45640
740-286-0071
www.richardmlewis.com

OKLAHOMA
Richard S. Shumberger, Esquire
1408 South Denver Avenue
Tulsa OK 74109
918-584-7600

Albert L. Wheeler, III
4200 Perimeter Center Drive, Suite 245
Oklahoma City OK 73112
405-946-2300
www.alwheelerlaw.com

OREGON
Scott Beckstead
Beeson & Beckstead, P.C.
236 West Olive Street
Newport OR 97365

PENNSYLVANIA
Barbara A. Ash
218A North 22nd Street
Philadelphia PA 19103
215-557-0395

Guy H. Brooks
Goldberg, Katzman & Shipman, P.C.
320 Market Street
Harrisburg PA 17108-1268
717-234-4161

Katherine H. Meehan
Eckell, Sparks, Levy, Auerbach, Monte, Rainer & Sloane
344 West Front Street
Media PA 19063
610-565-3700

RHODE ISLAND
Kathleen Managhan
Houlihan & Managhan, LLP
130 Bellevue Avenue, Suite 3
Newport RI 02840
401-846-7777
www.handmlaw.com

SOUTH CAROLINA
William J. LaLima
The Clekis Law Firm
171 Church Street, Suite 160
Charleston SC 29402
843-720-3737

TEXAS

Lyvonne Brittingham, Esquire
P.O. Box 780762
San Antonio TX 78278
210-823-9682
www.attorneyforpeopleandpets.com

Donald D. Feare, Jr.
721 West Division Street
Arlington TX 76012
817-543-2202

Helene G. Parker
Mosher Parker & Walter, LLP
1250 West Mockingbird Lane, Suite 125
Dallas TX 75247
214-267-9090
www.mpwlawfirm.com

VERMONT

Susan M. Ceglowski
Ceglowski & Thrasher, LLC
2023 Route 153
Rupert VT 05768
802-394-9944

VIRGINIA

Scott Nolan, Esquire
4122 Leonard Drive
Fairfax VA 22030
703-293-9095
www.nolanlaw.net

WASHINGTON, D.C.
Antilla E. Trotter, III
Sher & Blackwell LLP
1850 M Street, N.W., Suite 900
Washington DC 20036-5820
202-463-2500

WASHINGTON STATE
Adam Karp
600 First Avenue
Seattle WA 98104
206-903-1315
www.animal-lawyer.com

WEST VIRGINIA
Karen Kahle, Esquire
Steptoe & Johnson
P.O. Box 150
Wheeling WV 26003
304-233-0000
www.steptoelaw.com

WISCONSIN
P. Scott Hassett
Lawton & Cates, S.C.
10 East Doty Street, Suite 400
Madison WI 53701-2965
608-282-6200

Appendix C:
H.R. 1796

The following is the bill introduced by Representative Earl Blumenauer (D-OR) to legalize pet trusts in all 50 states.

To amend the Internal Revenue Code of 1986 to treat charitable remainder pet trusts in a similar manner as charitable remainder annuity trusts and charitable remainder unitrusts. (Introduced in House)

HR 1796 IH

107th CONGRESS
1st Session
H. R. 1796

To amend the Internal Revenue Code of 1986 to treat charitable remainder pet trusts in a similar manner as charitable remainder annuity trusts and charitable remainder unitrusts.

IN THE HOUSE OF REPRESENTATIVES
May 10, 2001

Mr. BLUMENAUER introduced the following bill; which was referred to the Committee on Ways and Means:

PerPETual Care

A BILL

To amend the Internal Revenue Code of 1986 to treat charitable remainder pet trusts in a similar manner as charitable remainder annuity trusts and charitable remainder unitrusts.

Be it enacted by the Senate and House of Representatives of the United States of America in Congress assembled,

SECTION 1. AMENDMENT OF 1986 CODE.
Except as otherwise expressly provided, whenever in this Act an amendment or repeal is expressed in terms of an amendment to, or repeal of, a section or other provision, the reference shall be considered to be made to a section or other provision of the Internal Revenue Code of 1986.

SECTION 2. CHARITABLE REMAINDER PET TRUSTS.
(a) CHARITABLE REMAINDER PET TRUST DEFINED–
Section 664(d) is amended by adding at the end the following new paragraphs:

`(5) CHARITABLE REMAINDER PET TRUST- For purposes of this section, a charitable remainder pet trust is a trust—

`(A) from which a sum certain is to be paid, not less often than annually, for the exclusive benefit of one or more pets (as defined in paragraph (6)) for a term of years (not in excess of 20 years) or for the life or lives of such pet or pets,

`(B) from which no amount other than the payments described in subparagraph (A) and the taxes imposed pursuant to subsection (c) may be paid to or for the use of any person other than an organization described in section 170(c),

`(C) following the termination of the payments described in subparagraph (A), the remainder interest in the trust is to be transferred to, or for the use of, an organization described in section 170(c), and

`(D) the value (determined under section 7520) of such remainder interest is at least 10 percent of the initial fair market value of all property placed in the trust.

`(6) PET- For purposes of a charitable remainder pet trust, a pet is any domesticated companion animal (including a domesticated companion cat, dog, rabbit, guinea pig, hamster, gerbil, ferret, mouse, rat, bird, fish, reptile, or horse) which is living, and owned or cared for by the taxpayer establishing the trust, at the time of the creation of the trust.'

(b) TAX ON ANNUITY DISTRIBUTIONS FROM CHARITABLE REMAINDER PET TRUSTS- Section 664(c) is amended by inserting ` and except, in the case of a charitable remainder pet trust, that any distribution during such year for the benefit of a pet (as defined in subsection (d)) shall be taxable income of the trust for such year, to the extent of the income of the trust for the year and undistributed income of the trust for prior years after `applied to such trust)'.

(c) CONFORMING AMENDMENTS–
(1) Section 170(f)(2)(A), section 2055(e)(2)(A), and section 2522(c)(2)(A) are amended by striking `charitable remainder annuity trust or a charitable remainder unitrust' and inserting `charitable remainder annuity trust, charitable remainder unitrust, or charitable remainder pet trust'.

(2) Subsections (a) and (c) of section 664 are amended by

striking `charitable remainder annuity trust and a charitable remainder unitrust' and inserting `charitable remainder annuity trust, charitable remainder unitrust, and charitable remainder pet trust'.

(3) Section 664(e) and section 1361(e)(1)(B)(iii) are amended by striking `charitable remainder annuity trust or charitable remainder unitrust' and inserting `charitable remainder annuity trust, charitable remainder unitrust, or charitable remainder pet trust'.

(4) Paragraphs (1) and (3) of section 664(f) are amended by striking `(1)(A) or (2)(A)' and inserting `(1)(A), (2)(A), or (5)(A)'.

(5) Section 2055(e)(2)(F) is amended by inserting `or pet (as defined in section 664(d))' after `by reason of the death of any individual'.

(6) Section 2652(c)(1)(C) is amended—
(A) in clause (ii) by striking `within the meaning of section 664, or' and inserting `,';

(B) by redesignating clause (iii) as clause (iv); and

(C) by inserting after clause (ii) the following new clause:
`(iii) a charitable remainder pet trust within the meaning of section 664, or'.

(d) EFFECTIVE DATE- The amendments made by this section shall apply to charitable remainder pet trusts created after the date of the enactment of this Act.

Appendix D:
Uniform Probate Code
Statute on Pet Trusts

The Uniform Probate Code was revised in 1990 by the National Conference of Commissioners on Uniform State Laws. The Conference consists of over 300 lawyers, judges and law professors, selected by state governments. This group's primary task is to develop proposed legal statutes for uniform and model laws in certain currently popular subjects, and to help legislatures to put the statutes into law.

Here is the sample code as drafted and accepted by the Conference in 1990. State legislatures are open to adopt the code as written, or adapt it for their own purposes.

14-2907. Honorary trusts; trusts for pets; conditions
A. If a trust is for a specific lawful noncharitable purpose or for lawful noncharitable purposes to be selected by the trustee and there is no definite or definitely ascertainable beneficiary designated, the trust may be performed by the trustee for not longer than twenty-one years whether or not the terms of the trust contemplate a longer duration.

B. A trust for the care of a designated domestic or pet animal is valid. The trust terminates when no living animal is covered by the trust. A governing instrument shall be liberally construed to bring the transfer within this subsection, to presume against the merely precatory or honorary nature of the disposition and to carry out the general intent of the transferor. Extrinsic evidence is admissible in determining the transferor's intent.

C. In addition to the provisions of subsection A or B, a trust created under this section is subject to the following:

1. Except as expressly provided otherwise in the trust instrument, no portion of the principal or income may be converted to the use of the trustee or to any use other than for the trust's purposes or for the benefit of a covered animal.

2. On termination, the trustee shall transfer the unexpended trust property in the following order:

(a) As directed in the trust instrument.

(b) If the trust was created in a nonresiduary clause in the transferor's will or in a codicil to the transferor's will, under the residuary clause in the transferor's will.

(c) If no taker is produced by the application of subdivision (a) or (b) of this paragraph, to the transferor's heirs under section 14-2711.

3. For the purposes of section 14-2707, the residuary clause is treated as creating a future interest under the terms of a trust.

4. The intended use of the principal or income can be enforced by a person who is designated for that purpose in

the trust instrument or, if none, by a person appointed by a court on application to it by any person.

5. Except as ordered by the court or required by the trust instrument, no filing, report, registration, periodic accounting, separate maintenance of funds, appointment or fee is required by reason of the existence of the fiduciary relationship of the trustee.

6. A court may reduce the amount of the property transferred if it determines that amount substantially exceeds the amount required for the intended use. The amount of the reduction, if any, passes as unexpended trust property under paragraph 2 of this subsection.

7. If no trustee is designated or no designated trustee is willing or able to serve, a court shall name a trustee. A court may order the transfer of the property to another trustee if this is necessary to assure that the intended use is carried out and if no successor trustee is designated in the trust instrument or if no designated successor trustee agrees to serve or is able to serve. A court may also make other orders and determinations that it determines advisable to carry out the intent of the transferor and this section.

Appendix E:
Pet Trusts
by State

What follows is a list of states that have passed statutes to legalize pet trusts along with the exact statutes. Some have accomplished the task in a paragraph or two, while others followed standard legislative procedure and wrote pages on the topic. Most have patterned their legislation after the Uniform Probate Code Statue on Pet Trusts detailed in Appendix D. These are current as of the summer of 2002. More states will undoubtedly be added to this list in future editions of *PerPETual Care*.

ALASKA
AS 13.12.907. Honorary Trusts; Trusts For Pets.
(a) Subject to (c) of this section, a trust may be performed by the trustee for 21 years but not longer, whether or not the terms of the trust contemplate a longer duration, if
(1) the trust is for a specific lawful, noncharitable purpose or for a lawful, noncharitable purpose to be selected by the trustee; and

(2) there is not a definite or definitely ascertainable beneficiary designated.

(b) Except as otherwise provided by this subsection and (c) of this section, a trust for the care of a designated domestic or pet animal is valid. The trust terminates when a living animal is not covered by the trust. A governing instrument shall be liberally construed to bring the transfer within this subsection, to presume against the merely precatory or honorary nature of the disposition, and to carry out the general intent of the transferor. Extrinsic evidence is admissible in determining the transferor's intent.

(c) In addition to the provisions of (a) or (b) of this section, a trust covered by either of those subsections is subject to the following provisions:

(1) except as expressly provided otherwise in the trust instrument, a portion of the principal or income may not be converted to the use of the trustee or to a use other than for the trust's purposes or for the benefit of a covered animal;

(2) upon termination, the trustee shall transfer the unexpended trust property in the following order:

(A) as directed in the trust instrument;

(B) if the trust was created in a nonresiduary clause in the transferor's will or in a codicil to the transferor's will, under the residuary clause in the transferor's will; and

(C) if a taker is not produced by the application of (A) or (B) of this paragraph, to the transferor's heirs under AS 13.12.711;

(3) for the purposes of AS 13.12.707, the residuary clause is treated as creating a future interest under the terms of a trust;

(4) the intended use of the principal or income may be enforced by an individual designated for that purpose in the trust instrument or, if none, by an individual appointed by a

court upon application to the court by an individual;

(5) except as ordered by the court or required by the trust instrument, a filing, report, registration, periodic accounting, separate maintenance of funds, appointment, or fee is not required by reason of the existence of the fiduciary relationship of the trustee;

(6) a court may reduce the amount of the property transferred, if it determines that amount substantially exceeds the amount required for the intended use; the amount of the reduction, if any, passes as unexpended trust property under (2) of this subsection;

(7) if a trustee is not designated or a designated trustee is not willing or able to serve, a court shall name a trustee; a court may order the transfer of the property to another trustee, if required to assure that the intended use is carried out and if a successor trustee is not designated in the trust instrument or if a designated successor trustee does not agree to serve or is unable to serve; a court may also make other orders and determinations as are advisable to carry out the intent of the transferor and the purpose of this section.

ARIZONA

14-2907. Honorary trusts; trusts for pets; conditions

A. If a trust is for a specific lawful noncharitable purpose or for lawful noncharitable purposes to be selected by the trustee and there is no definite or definitely ascertainable beneficiary designated, the trust may be performed by the trustee for not longer than twenty-one years whether or not the terms of the trust contemplate a longer duration.

B. A trust for the care of a designated domestic or pet animal is valid. The trust terminates when no living animal is covered by the trust. A governing instrument shall be liberally construed to bring the transfer within this subsection, to presume against the merely precatory or honorary nature of the disposition and to carry out the general intent of the transferor. Extrinsic evidence is admissible in determining the transferor's intent.

C. In addition to the provisions of subsection A or B, a trust created under this section is subject to the following:

1. Except as expressly provided otherwise in the trust instrument, no portion of the principal or income may be converted to the use of the trustee or to any use other than for the trust's purposes or for the benefit of a covered animal.

2. On termination, the trustee shall transfer the unexpended trust property in the following order:

(a) As directed in the trust instrument.

(b) If the trust was created in a nonresiduary clause in the transferor's will or in a codicil to the transferor's will, under the residuary clause in the transferor's will.

(c) If no taker is produced by the application of subdivision (a) or (b) of this paragraph, to the transferor's heirs under section 14-2711.

3. For the purposes of section 14-2707, the residuary clause is treated as creating a future interest under the terms of a trust.

4. The intended use of the principal or income can be enforced by a person who is designated for that purpose in the trust instrument or, if none, by a person appointed by a court on application to it by any person.

5. Except as ordered by the court or required by the trust instrument, no filing, report, registration, periodic accounting, separate maintenance of funds, appointment or fee is required by reason of the existence of the fiduciary relationship of the trustee.

6. A court may reduce the amount of the property trans-

ferred if it determines that amount substantially exceeds the amount required for the intended use. The amount of the reduction, if any, passes as unexpended trust property under paragraph 2 of this subsection.

7. If no trustee is designated or no designated trustee is willing or able to serve, a court shall name a trustee. A court may order the transfer of the property to another trustee if this is necessary to assure that the intended use is carried out and if no successor trustee is designated in the trust instrument or if no designated successor trustee agrees to serve or is able to serve. A court may also make other orders and determinations that it determines advisable to carry out the intent of the transferor and this section.

CALIFORNIA

15212. A trust for the care of a designated domestic or pet animal may be performed by the trustee for the life of the animal, whether or not there is a beneficiary who can seek enforcement or termination of the trust and whether or not the terms of the trust contemplate a longer duration.

COLORADO

15-11-901 - Honorary trusts; trusts for pets.

(1) Honorary trust. Subject to subsection (3) of this section, and except as provided under sections 38-30-110, 38-30-111, and 38-30-112, C.R.S., if (i) a trust is for a specific, lawful, noncharitable purpose or for lawful, noncharitable purposes to be selected by the trustee and (ii) there is no definite or definitely ascertainable beneficiary designated, the trust may be performed by the trustee for twenty-one years but no longer, whether or not the terms of the trust contemplate a

longer duration.

(2) Trust for pets. Subject to this subsection (2) and subsection (3) of this section, a trust for the care of designated domestic or pet animals and the animals' offspring in gestation is valid. For purposes of this subsection (2), the determination of the "animals' offspring in gestation" is made at the time the designated domestic or pet animals become present beneficiaries of the trust. Unless the trust instrument provides for an earlier termination, the trust terminates when no living animal is covered by the trust. A governing instrument shall be liberally construed to bring the transfer within this subsection (2), to presume against the merely precatory or honorary nature of the disposition, and to carry out the general intent of the transferor. Extrinsic evidence is admissible in determining the transferor's intent. Any trust under this subsection (2) shall be an exception to any statutory or common law rule against perpetuities.

(3) Additional provisions applicable to honorary trusts and trusts for pets. In addition to the provisions of subsection (1) or (2) of this section, a trust covered by either of those subsections is subject to the following provisions:

(a) Except as expressly provided otherwise in the trust instrument, no portion of the principal or income may be converted to the use of the trustee, other than reasonable trustee fees and expenses of administration, or to any use other than for the trust's purposes or for the benefit of a covered animal or animals.

(b) Upon termination, the trustee shall transfer the unexpended trust property in the following order:

(I) As directed in the trust instrument;

(II) If the trust was created in a nonresiduary clause in the transferor's will or in a codicil to the transferor's will, under the residuary clause in the transferor's will; and

(III) If no taker is produced by the application of subparagraph (I) or (II) of this paragraph (b), to the transferor's heirs under part 5 of this article.

(c) (Reserved)

(d) The intended use of the principal or income can be enforced by an individual designated for that purpose in the trust instrument, by the person having custody of an animal for which care is provided by the trust instrument, by a remainder beneficiary, or, if none, by an individual appointed by a court upon application to it by an individual.

(e) All trusts created under this section shall be registered and all trustees shall be subject to the laws of this state applying to trusts and trustees.

(f) (Reserved)

(g) If no trustee is designated or no designated trustee is willing or able to serve, a court shall name a trustee. A court may order the transfer of the property to another trustee, if required to assure that the intended use is carried out and if no successor trustee is designated in the trust instrument or if no designated successor trustee agrees to serve or is able to serve. A court may also make such other orders and determinations as shall be advisable to carry out the intent of the transferor and the purpose of this section.

MICHIGAN

Act 386 of 1998

700.2722 Honorary trusts; trusts for pets.

Sec. 2722. (1) Subject to subsection (3), if a trust is for a specific lawful noncharitable purpose or for lawful noncharitable purposes to be selected by the trustee, and if there is no definite or definitely ascertainable beneficiary designated, the trust may be performed by the trustee for 21 years, but no longer, whether or not the terms of the trust contemplate a longer duration.

(2) Subject to this subsection and subsection (3), a trust for the care of a designated domestic or pet animal is valid. The trust terminates when no living animal is covered by the trust. A governing instrument shall be liberally construed to bring the transfer within this subsection, to presume against the merely precatory or honorary nature of the disposition, and to carry out the general intent of the transferor. Extrinsic evidence is admissible in determining the transferor's intent.

(3) In addition to the provisions of subsection (1) or (2), a trust covered by either of those subsections is subject to the following provisions: (a) Except as expressly provided otherwise in the trust instrument, no portion of the principal or income may be converted to the use of the trustee or to a use other than for the trust's purposes or for the benefit of a covered animal.

(b) Upon termination, the trustee shall transfer the unexpended trust property in the following order: (i) As directed in the trust instrument.

(ii) If the trust was created in a nonresiduary clause in the transferor's will or in a codicil to the transferor's will, under the residuary clause in the transferor's will.

(iii) If no taker is produced by the application of subparagraph (i) or (ii), to the transferor's heirs under section 2720.

(c) For the purposes of sections 2714 to 2716, the residuary clause is treated as creating a future interest under the terms of a trust.

(d) The intended use of the principal or income can be enforced by an individual designated for that purpose in the trust instrument or, if none, by an individual appointed by a court upon petition to it by an individual.

(e) Except as ordered by the court or required by the trust instrument, no filing, report, registration, periodic accounting, separate maintenance of funds, appointment, or fee is required by reason of the existence of the fiduciary relationship of the trustee.

(f) The court may reduce the amount of the property transferred if it determines that that amount substantially exceeds the amount required for the intended use. The amount of the reduction, if any, passes as unexpended trust property under subdivision (b).

(g) If a trustee is not designated or no designated trustee is willing or able to serve, the court shall name a trustee. The court may order the transfer of the property to another trustee if the transfer is necessary to ensure that the intended use is carried out, and if a successor trustee is not designated in the trust instrument or if no designated successor trustee agrees to serve or is able to serve. The court may also make other orders and determinations as are advisable to carry out the intent of the transferor and the purpose of this section.

(h) The trust is not subject to the uniform statutory rule against perpetuities, 1988 PA 418, MCL 554.71 to 554.78.

History: 1998, Act 386, Eff. Apr. 1, 2000.

MISSOURI

Chapter 456

August 28, 2001

Honorary trusts – pet animals noncharitable societies.

456.055. A trust for care of pet animals or other lawful specific noncharitable purpose, society or organization may be carried out by the intended trustee or a successor trustee for twenty-one years or any shorter period specified by the terms of the trust although it has no ascertainable human beneficiary or might, by its terms, last longer than the period of the rule against perpetuities.

MONTANA

72-2-1017. Honorary trusts – trusts for pets.

(1) Subject to subsection (3), a trust may be performed by the trustee for 21 years but no longer, whether or not the terms of the trust contemplate a longer duration if:

(a) a trust is for a specific lawful noncharitable purpose or for lawful noncharitable purposes to be selected by the trustee; and

(b) there is no definite or definitely ascertainable beneficiary designated.

(2) Subject to the provisions of subsection (3) and this subsection, a trust for the care of a designated domestic or pet animal is valid. The trust terminates when no living animal is covered by the trust. A governing instrument must be liberally construed to bring the transfer within this subsection, to presume against the merely precatory or honorary nature of the disposition, and to carry out the general intent of the transferor. Extrinsic evidence is admissible in determining the transferor's intent.

(3) In addition to the provisions of subsection (1) or (2), a trust covered by either of those subsections is subject to the following provisions:

(a) Except as expressly provided otherwise in the trust instrument, no portion of the principal or income may be converted to the use of the trustee or to any use other than for the trust's purposes or for the benefit of a covered animal.

(b) Upon termination, the trustee shall transfer the unexpended trust property in the following order:

(i) as directed in the trust instrument;

(ii) if the trust was created in a nonresiduary clause in the transferor's will or in a codicil to the transferor's will, under the residuary clause in the transferor's will; and

(iii) if no taker is produced by the application of subsection (3)(b)(i) or (3)(b)(ii), to the transferor's heirs under 72-2-721.

(c) For the purposes of 72-2-717, the residuary clause is treated as creating a future interest under the terms of a trust.

(d) The intended use of the principal or income may be enforced by an individual designated for that purpose in the trust instrument or, if none, by an individual appointed by a court upon application to it by an individual.

(e) Except as ordered by the court or required by the trust instrument, no filing, report, registration, periodic accounting, separate maintenance of funds, appointment, or fee is required by reason of the existence of the fiduciary relationship of the trustee.

(f) A court may reduce the amount of the property transferred if it determines that that amount substantially exceeds the amount required for the intended use. The amount of the reduction, if any, passes as unexpended trust property under subsection (3)(b).

(g) If no trustee is designated or no designated trustee is willing or able to serve, a court shall name a trustee. A court may order the transfer of the property to another trustee if required to ensure that the intended use is carried out and if no successor trustee is designated in the trust instrument or if no designated successor trustee agrees to serve or is able to serve. A court may also make such other orders and determinations as are advisable to carry out the intent of the transferor and the purpose of this section.

NEW MEXICO

45-2-907. Honorary trusts; trusts for pets.

A. Subject to Subsection C of this section, if (i) a trust is for a specific lawful noncharitable purpose or for lawful noncharitable purposes to be selected by the trustee and (ii) there is no definite or definitely ascertainable beneficiary designated, the trust may be performed by the trustee for twenty-one years but no longer, whether or not the terms of the trust contemplate a longer duration.

B. Subject to this subsection and Subsection C of this section, a trust for the care of a designated domestic or pet animal is valid. The trust terminates when no living animal is covered by the trust. A governing instrument shall be liberally construed to bring the transfer within this subsection, to presume against the merely precatory or honorary nature of the disposition, and to carry out the general intent of the transferor. Extrinsic evidence is admissible in determining the transferor's intent.

C. In addition to the provisions of Subsection A or B of this section, a trust covered by either of those subsections is subject to the following provisions:

(1) except as expressly provided otherwise in the trust instrument, no portion of the principal or income may be converted to the use of the trustee or to any use other than for the trust's purposes or for the benefit of a covered animal;

(2) upon termination, the trustee shall transfer the unexpended trust property in the following order:

(a) as directed in the trust instrument;

(b) if the trust was created in a nonresiduary clause in the transferor's will or in a codicil to the transferor's will, under the residuary clause in the transferor's will; and

(c) if no taker is produced by the application of Subparagraph (a) or (b), to the transferor's heirs under the provisions of

APPENDIX E

Section 45-2-711 NMSA 1978;

(3) for the purposes of Section 45-2-707 NMSA 1978, the residuary clause is treated as creating a future interest under the terms of a trust;

(4) the intended use of the principal or income can be enforced by an individual designated for that purpose in the trust instrument or, if none, by an individual appointed by a court upon application to it by an individual;

(5) except as ordered by the court or required by the trust instrument, no filing, report, registration, periodic accounting, separate maintenance of funds, appointment or fee is required by reason of the existence of the fiduciary relationship of the trustee;

(6) a court may reduce the amount of the property transferred, if it determines that amount substantially exceeds the amount required for the intended use. The amount of the reduction, if any, passes as unexpended trust property under the provisions of Paragraph (2) of Subsection C of this section; and

(7) if no trustee is designated or no designated trustee is willing or able to serve, a court shall name a trustee. A court may order the transfer of the property to another trustee, if required to assure that the intended use is carried out and if no successor trustee is designated in the trust instrument or if no designated successor trustee agrees to serve or is able to serve. A court may also make such other orders and determinations as shall be advisable to carry out the intent of the transferor and the purpose of this section.

NEW YORK
§ 7-6.1 Honorary trusts for pets
(a) A trust for the care of a designated domestic or pet ani-

mal is valid. The intended use of the principal or income may be enforced by an individual designated for that purpose in the trust instrument or, if none, by an individual appointed by a court upon application to it by an individual, or by a trustee. Such trust shall terminate when no living animal is covered by the trust, or at the end of twenty-one years, whichever occurs earlier.

(b) Except as expressly provided otherwise in the trust instrument, no portion of the principal or income may be converted to the use of the trustee or to any use other than for the benefit of a covered animal.

(c) Upon termination, the trustee shall transfer the unexpended trust property as directed in the trust instrument or, if there are no such directions in the trust instrument, the property shall pass to the estate of the grantor.

(d) A court may reduce the amount of the property transferred if it determines that amount substantially exceeds the amount required for the intended use. The amount of the reduction, if any, passes as unexpended trust property pursuant to paragraph (c) of this section.

(e) If no trustee is designated or no designated trustee is willing or able to serve, a court shall appoint a trustee and may make such other orders and determinations as are advisable to carry out the intent of the transferor and the purpose of this section.

NORTH CAROLINA

§ 36A-147. Trusts for pets.

(a) Subject to the provisions of this section, a trust for the care of one or more designated domestic or pet animals alive at the time of creation of the trust is valid.

(b) Except as expressly provided otherwise in the trust instrument, no portion of the principal or income may be converted to the use of the trustee or to any use other than for the benefit of the designated animal or animals.

(c) The trust terminates at the death of the animal or last surviving animal. Upon termination, the trustee shall transfer the unexpended trust property in the following order:

(1) As directed in the trust instrument;

(2) If the trust was created in a preresiduary clause in the transferor's will or in a codicil to the transferor's will, under the residuary clause in the transferor's will;

(3) If no taker is produced by the application of subdivision (1) or (2) of this subsection, to the transferor or the transferor's heirs determined as of the date of the transferor's death under Chapter 29 of the General Statutes.

(d) The intended use of the principal or income can be enforced by an individual designated for that purpose in the trust instrument or, if none, by an individual appointed by the clerk of superior court having jurisdiction over the decedent's estate upon application to the clerk by an individual.

(e) Except as ordered by the clerk or required by the trust instrument, no filing, report, registration, periodic accounting, separate maintenance of funds, appointment, bond, or fee is required by reason of the existence of the fiduciary relationship of the trustee.

(f) A governing instrument shall be liberally construed to bring the transfer within this section, to presume against the merely precatory or honorary nature of the disposition, and to carry out the general intent of the transferor. Extrinsic evidence shall be admissible in determining the transferor's intent.

(g) The clerk may reduce the amount of the property transferred, if the clerk determines that the amount substantially exceeds the amount required for the intended use. The amount of the reduction, if any, passes as unexpended trust property under subsection (c) of this section.

(h) If no trustee is designated or if no designated trustee agrees to serve or is able to serve, the clerk shall name a trustee. The clerk may order the transfer of the property to another trustee, if required to assure that the intended use is carried out and if no successor trustee is designated in the trust instrument or if no designated successor trustee agrees to serve or is able to serve. The clerk may also make such other orders and determinations as shall be advisable to carry out the intent of the transferor and the purpose of this section. (1995, c. 225, s. 1.)

OREGON

Chapter 636 Oregon Laws 2001
AN ACT
SB 166
Be It Enacted by the People of the State of Oregon:
SECTION 1. (1) Any person may establish a pet trust for the care of designated domestic or pet animals. A pet trust may provide for the care of individually named animals or for a class of animals, but any animal provided for under the trust must be living at the time of the trustor's death. Wills and other instruments shall be liberally construed in favor of finding the creation of a pet trust, and there is a presumption against merely precatory or honorary disposition on behalf of domestic and pet animals.

(2) The terms and conditions of a pet trust may be enforced by an individual designated for that purpose in the trust instrument. If the trust instrument does not designate a person to enforce the terms and conditions of the pet trust, the circuit court may appoint a person for that purpose. Reasonable

compensation for a person appointed by the court may be paid from the assets of the trust.

(3) If a trustee is not designated in a pet trust or the person designated to act as trustee is unwilling or unable to serve, the circuit court shall name a trustee. A pet trust may designate one or more persons to serve as successor trustee. The court may order the transfer of the property to a person other than the designated trustee or successor trustee if the transfer is required to ensure that the trustor's intent is carried out. The court may also make such other orders as the court deems necessary to carry out the intent of the trustor and the purposes of this section.

(4) Upon termination of a pet trust, the trustee shall transfer the unexpended trust property in the following order:

(a) As directed by the trust instrument;

(b) If the trust was created in a nonresiduary clause in the trustor's will, under the residuary clause in the trustor's will; or

(c) If paragraphs (a) and (b) of this subsection do not apply, to the persons to whom the estate of the trustor would pass by intestate succession under ORS 112.025 to 112.055.

(5) Except as ordered by a circuit court or required by the trust instrument, no filing, report, registration, periodic accounting, separate maintenance of funds, appointment or fee is required by reason of the existence of the fiduciary relationship of the trustee.

(6) A pet trust terminates as provided by the terms of the trust instrument. If the trust instrument makes no provision for termination of the trust, the trust terminates when no living animal is covered by the trust or when all trust assets are exhausted, whichever occurs first.

TENNESSEE

35-50-118. Trusts for care of animals

(a) Any gift or devise under a will or trust having as its object the humane treatment and care of a specific animal or animals designated by the donor and testator shall be valid, even though it creates a perpetuity in such animal or animals, or creates a condition subsequent that must be fulfilled before a person is entitled to the outright receipt of the gift or devise. Such gift or devise shall be considered an honorary trust, that is, one binding the conscience of the trustee, since there is no beneficiary capable of enforcing such a trust.

(b) Such gift or devise shall provide for the appointment of a trustee to carry out the provisions of the trust, but in the event that no trustee or successor trustee is named, the person designated as donee or devisee of such gift or devise, or in the case such person is a minor, then the minor's court-appointed representative, shall serve as trustee and hold such property in trust for the benefit of such animal or animals.

(c) Any such trust shall terminate and any conditions shall be extinguished on the death of such animal or animals or as provided for by will or trust, but in all events, any such trust shall terminate twenty-one (21) years after the death of the donor or testator

UTAH

75-2-1001. Honorary trusts – Trusts for pets.

(1) Subject to Subsection (3), if a trust is for a specific lawful noncharitable purpose or for a lawful noncharitable purpose to be selected by the trustee and there is no definite or definitely ascertainable beneficiary designated, the trust may be performed by the trustee for 21 years but no longer whether or not the terms of the trust contemplate a longer duration.

(2) Subject to this subsection and Subsection (3), a trust for the care of a designated domestic or pet animal is valid. The trust terminates when no living animal is covered by the trust. A governing instrument shall be liberally construed to bring the transfer within this subsection, to presume against the merely precatory or honorary nature of the disposition, and to carry out the general intent of the transferor. Extrinsic evidence is admissible in determining the transferor's intent.

(3) In addition to the provisions of Subsection (a) or (b), a trust covered by either of those subsections is subject to the following provisions:

(a) Except as expressly provided otherwise in the trust instrument, no portion of the principle or income may be converted to the use of the trustee or to any use other than for the trust's purposes or for the benefit of a covered animal.

(b) Upon termination, the trustee shall transfer the unexpended trust property in the following order:

(i) as directed in the trust instrument;

(ii) if the trust was created in a nonresiduary clause in the transferor's will or in a codicil to the transferor's will, under the residuary clause in the transferor's will; and

(iii) if no taker is produced by the application of Subsection (i) or (ii), to the transferor's heirs under Section 75-2-711.

(c) For the purposes of Section 75-2-707, the residuary clause is treated as creating a future interest under the terms of a trust.

(d) The intended use of the principal or income can be enforced by an individual designated for that purpose in the trust instrument or, if none, by an individual appointed by a court upon application to it by an individual.

(e) Except as ordered by the court or required by the trust instrument, no filing, report, registration, periodic accounting, separate maintenance of funds, appointment, or fee is required by reason of the existence of the fiduciary relationship of the trustee.

(f) A court may reduce the amount of the property transferred, if it determines that that amount substantially exceeds the amount required for the intended use. The amount of the reduction, if any, passes as unexpended trust property under Subsection (b).

(g) If no trustee is designated or no designated trustee is willing or able to serve, a court shall name a trustee. A court may order the transfer of the property to another trustee, if required to assure that the intended use is carried out and if no successor trustee is designated in the trust instrument or if no designated successor trustee agrees to serve or is able to serve. A court may also make such other orders and determinations as shall be advisable to carry out the intent of the transferor and the purpose of this section.

WISCONSIN

701.11 Honorary trusts.

(1) Except under sub. (2), where the owner of property makes a testamentary transfer in trust for a specific noncharitable purpose, and there is no definite or definitely ascertainable human beneficiary designated, no enforceable trust is created; but the transferee has power to apply the property to the designated purpose, unless the purpose is capricious. If the transferee refuses or neglects to apply the property to the designated purpose within a reasonable time and the transferor has not manifested an intention to make a beneficial gift to the transferee, a resulting trust arises in favor of the transferor's estate and the court is authorized to order the transferee to retransfer the property.

Appendix F:
Sample Pet Trust

What follows is one example of a pet trust, drafted by Miriam Abrams Goodman, Esquire, of Frascona, Joiner, Goodman, and Greenstein, P.C., in Boulder, Colorado (www.frascona.com). I include it with the following disclaimer, courtesy of Attorney Goodman:

"This trust language is printed for illustrative purposes only and does not constitute legal advice or establish an attorney-client relationship; please consult your own estate-planning attorney to prepare documents appropriate for your situation. Trust and estate laws vary significantly from state to state."

XYZ PET TRUST
The XYZ Pet Trust shall be held and administered as follows:

1.1   PAYMENT OF MORTGAGES ON RESIDENCE: My trustee shall first apply trust assets to pay off all mortgages on my residence, which at this time is at xxxx   (hereafter, "my residence").

1.2 ESTABLISHMENT OF ENDOWMENT FUND: My trustee shall next set aside as an endowment fund an amount of property sufficient to generate income for the purposes set forth in paragraph 1.4 below, for the lifetime of all animals I owned or cared for at the time of my death, plus the life of any offspring of such animals in gestation at the time of my death (hereafter, "my animals").

My trustee may add to the fund such amount as the trustee determines to be a reasonable cushion against unforeseeable circumstances incident to carrying out the purposes of the trust, such amount not to exceed twenty five percent (25%) of the amount my trustee determines to be necessary to carry out the purposes of the trust.

My trustee shall set the amount of this fund no later than two (2) years after my death based upon the trustee's experience carrying out the purposes of this trust during those two years; provided, however, that if my caretaker or trustee incurs legal expenses to enforce the XYZ Pet Trust, my trustee shall set the amount of the fund after such expenses are finalized and reimbursed from the trust estate.

This endowment fund shall be designated and hereafter referred to as "The XYZ Pet Trust."

1.3 DISTRIBUTION OF EXCESS TRUST FUNDS: My trustee shall distribute any trust funds in excess of that amount necessary to establish the XYZ Pet Trust to the following beneficiaries; however, before making such distributions my trustee shall obtain from each donee a written release of any claims or challenges to the validity of the XYZ Pet Trust. With regard to the XYZ Educational Fund, my trustee shall obtain such release from each adult beneficiary of such trust, and from the guardian of each minor beneficiary of such trust.

(A)   Fifteen percent (15%) to my spouse's brother xxx; if xxx does not survive me, this gift shall pass to his issue by representation. If xxx survives me and disclaims this gift in the time and manner provided by law, this gift shall pass to the XYZ Educational Trust established under this will.

(B)   Fifteen percent (15%) to remain in trust as the XYZ Educational Trust, to be administered in accordance with the provisions of Article 6. Any portion of the XYZ Educational Trust which, by reason of a person's attained age, death or otherwise, would have become distributable before the establishment of a separate fund, may be distributed directly by trustee without requiring that such a separate fund be established or that distribution be made by trustee of such separate fund.

(C)   Five percent (5%) to xxx; if xxx does not survive me, this gift shall be distributed in proportional shares to the remaining beneficiaries listed in this paragraph 1.3.
(additional contingent specific and charitable gifts go here)

1.4 ADMINISTRATION OF XYZ PET TRUST:
 (A)   Appointment of Caretaker: I appoint John Doe of Lakewood, Colorado as the caretaker of my residence and animals. I designate my caretaker as the person entitled to enforce the intended use of the principal or income of the XYZ Pet Trust pursuant to Colorado Revised Statutes §15-11-901(3)(d), as amended. If John Doe fails or ceases to act as caretaker for any reason, I appoint Jane Smith of Longmont,

Colorado as successor caretaker.

(B)   Rights of Caretaker: My caretaker shall own my animals, which I leave to his (or her, in the case of my successor) kind care and judgment, and he or she shall live in my
residence rent-free, both for as long as he or she serves as
caretaker of my animals. My caretaker shall pay all his or her
own personal living expenses, including but not limited to all
utilities, propane, phone, and other services not exclusively
required by my animals. My caretaker also shall be responsible for repairs to my residence caused by any use which exceeds the bounds of ordinary wear and tear on the property. My trustee's determination as to whether an expense is
personal to the caretaker or a trust expense shall be conclu-
sive on all persons. My caretaker shall maintain reasonable
communications with my trustee so my trustee is informed
in a timely manner of necessary maintenance and other
property expenses.

(C)   Distributions of Income And Principal: My trustee
shall distribute to my caretaker, or directly apply for the
benefit of my animals, such amounts of the net income or
principal, or both, as my trustee determines, in its discretion,
to be necessary or advisable for care of my animals. Such
care shall take into account the animals' living standard at
my death, and includes but is not limited to costs for food,
medical care, and burial of such animals' remains, which
shall be adjacent to the other XYZ pet burial plots, [e.g., under the large tree in the front yard of my residence, near the
satellite dish].

My trustee also shall apply trust income and principal as
my trustee, in my trustee's discretion, shall determine to be

necessary or advisable for maintenance of my residence in good saleable condition. Such maintenance shall include taxes, insurance, upkeep, and any other expense for the reasonable care of the residence necessary to provide housing for my animals and their caretaker and to carry out the other purposes of this trust.

My trustee also shall apply trust income and principal for any legal expenses incurred by my trustee or my caretaker which are necessary to enforce the purposes of the XYZ Pet Trust.

Any income not distributed may be added periodically to principal. Although the Fund is intended as an endowment, I authorize my trustee to distribute principal where necessary to achieve the purposes of the trust, keeping in mind the probable future expenses of the trust and the size of the cushion established at the outset of the fund. I do not intend that my trustee borrow money or mortgage my residence to provide income for the purposes of the trust.

(D)   Termination of XYZ Pet Trust: The XYZ Pet Trust shall terminate upon any of the following events:

(1) My last appointed successor caretaker resigns or fails to serve as caretaker for any reason.
(2) All my animals have deceased.
(3) My last appointed successor caretaker gives my trustee written notice of such caretaker's intention to vacate my residence.

Upon any of these termination events, my trustee shall, within 60 days, notify my then-serving caretaker in writing that the trust has been terminated. If such caretaker has served as caretaker until all my animals are deceased (regardless of when such caretaker began serving), my trustee shall also notify such caretaker that such caretaker may purchase my residence at seventy-five percent (75%) of its fair market value. This option price shall be determined by a qualified appraiser selected by my trustee and shall be included in the notice of termination. Within sixty (60) days of the date such notice of termination was mailed by my trustee, such caretaker shall exercise the option to purchase granted herein by notifying my trustee, in a writing delivered to the trustee, of his or her intent to purchase my residence. Such writing shall include evidence of such caretaker's ability to finance such purchase. If my caretaker has terminated the trust before all my animals have deceased, or if my caretaker fails to exercise this option in the time and manner specified, my trustee shall sell my residence on the open market, giving preference in the order received to offers made by any relative or friend of mine or my spouse mentioned in my will. My trustee shall add the proceeds of sale of my residence to any assets or funds remaining in the XYZ Pet Trust, and shall distribute the balance as follows:

If any of my animals are living at the time of termination, I give them to my last serving caretaker.

Resources

Admittedly, before *PerPETual Care: Who Will Look After Your Pets If You're Not Around* was introduced, available resources on the topic of planning for your pets' future was pretty slim. Following are the resources that I found to be particularly valuable in researching and writing this book, and that I felt I could wholeheartedly recommend to any pet lover in the process of planning for PerPETual Care. Hopefully, this section will be expanded by the next edition of this book is published.

BOOKS

Everett, Jack W. *The Truth About Trusts: A Trustee's Survival Guide.* FTPC Publishing, 1999.

Sitarz, Daniel. *Prepare Your Own Will: The National Will Kit.* Carbondale, Illinois: Nova Publishing Company, 2000.

BROCHURES

Providing For Your Pet's Future Without You
Humane Society of the United States.
Washington, D.C.
www.hsus.org

Websites
Pet Trusts: Providing for Pets
Gerhard Shipley, J.D.
www.keln.org/bibs/shipley.html

Tax and Estate Planning Involving Pets: Stupid Pet Tricks for
the IRS and FIDO
J. Alan Jensen, J.D.
www.weiss-law.com/Pet_Tricks.htm

Estate Planning for Non-Human Family Members
Gerry W. Beyer, Professor of Law
St. Mary's University School of Law
San Antonio, Texas
www.professorbeyer.com/Articles/Animals.htm

Association of the Bar of the City of New York
"Providing for Your Pets in the Event of Your Death or Hos-
pitalization."
On the homepage, click on Reports/Publications, then on
Brochures, scroll down and you'll find the above report.
www.abcny.org

Index

INDEX

INDEX

WWW.LITTERATURE.COM

SYMPATHY CARDS
ADOPTION ANNOUNCEMENTS
THANK YOU CARDS
AND MORE...

ORDER FORM

You can purchase additional copies of *PerPETual Care* from Amazon, ask your local bookstore, or order from us directly.

Fax: 603-523-7663

Phone: 800-639-1099 (orders only, please)

Web: www.PerPETualCarebook.com (secure ordering)

Email: orders@PerPETualCarebook.com

Mail: Litterature, 212 Kinsman Road, Grafton NH 03240

☐ Please send me ____ copies of PerPETual Care at $15 each, plus shipping and handling.

☐ Please contact me about buying wholesale copies of PerPETual Care for resale or for nonprofit fundraising.

Name_____

Organization_____

Address_____

City/State/Zip_____

Phone_____

Email address_____

Shipping: U.S. $4 for the first book, $2 for each additional book. No sales tax. For international & Canadian orders, email for shipping rate.

Payment type: ☐ Check/money order ☐ Visa ☐ MasterCard

☐ American Express

Credit card #_____

Name on card_____ Exp date_____

Signature_____